RANTS, RAVES
& Recollections

Rafe Mair

WHITECAP BOOKS

TORONTO/VANCOUVER

"Out of the Shadows" was originally printed in an issue of *Elm Street* magazine and
is reproduced here with their kind permission.

Edited by Carolyn Bateman
Proofread by Elizabeth Salomons
Design by Roberta Batchelor

Printed in Canada

Canadian Cataloguing in Publication Data

Mair, Rafe, 1931–
    Rants, raves and recollections

    ISBN 1-55285-145-1

    I. Title.
AC8.M315 2000   081   C00-911073-9

The publisher acknowledges the support of the Canada Council for the Arts and the
Cultural Services Branch of the Government of British Columbia for our publishing
program. We acknowledge the financial support of the Government of Canada through
the Book Industry Development Program for our publishing activities.

To the late Melvin H. Smith, QC, a great British Columbian and Canadian for whom the words of Cato the Elder are so apt: "I would much rather have men ask why I have no statue than why I have one."

Contents

INTRODUCTION

George Gershwin once said that he had a million tunes running around in his head. I could certainly not make that claim. The only tune I ever have running around in my head is some damned thing I've heard and can't seem to shake. But I have always had lots and lots of thoughts. As a child I used to wonder a lot—I guess we all do as kids—but I never broke the habit and I have often found in my adult life that my mind will be wondering, and wandering, just when I should be concentrating on the task at hand. I'm lucky in that I have made my living for the past twenty years by having thoughts and putting them down on paper or for broadcast. I write five editorials a week for my radio show, plus three articles per week for publication, plus perhaps a dozen or more per year for publication elsewhere. On top of that, I am expected, on the open-line segments of my radio show, as on the ad hoc TV I do, to express thoughts extemporaneously. I'm also very lucky that since 1960 I have always worked at some-thing where Monday morning was something I very much looked forward to.

This book is about thoughts. They have not been used or published elsewhere with the exception of "Out of the Shadows" from *Elm Street* magazine, an article that continued to generate mail a year after it was published. Perhaps a half-dozen of these pieces have been published in part on my website, www.rafeonline.com, but unless you were one of the forty subscribers at the time they were published you won't have read them. And perhaps not even then!

Thoughts are difficult to distinguish from day dreams—

perhaps when all's said and done they're not different at all. And the fact that I've always been a day dreamer may have led me into the rather curious career path I've wandered down for nearly half a century and could account for the fact that I was—and hopefully still am—a late bloomer. For as I look back I see a moderately successful lawyer in Vancouver and Kamloops rather suddenly in a position of power as a provincial cabinet minister, then perhaps with even more influence as a journalist and wonder how I got where I am. Was there anything in earlier days that marked me as a person who might have some impact as a broadcaster and writer?

I was always good in English and did as a child receive a prize for a bit of wartime fiction I called "The Poppin Bay Mystery" but apart from the odd letter to the editor of a local newspaper or the lawyers' trade paper, *The Advocate*, I expressed very little by way of original thought until the 1980s when I had passed the half-century mark.

But there was a moment that, in hindsight, turned me to journalism. (I use that term very loosely remembering that Denny Boyd, during the Charlottetown Referendum campaign, made it clear that I wasn't a journalist but a cross-examiner.) It happened in 1979.

As the MLA for Kamloops I wrote a weekly article for the two local papers. Most columns were the usual political drivel one comes to expect from politicians. On one occasion, after a trip to Japan in 1979, I wrote as my regular article a piece called "Everyone Should Visit Hiroshima." It was, I say modestly, a damn good piece and reflected all the awe and horror I felt after visiting the first of two cities to have been demolished by the atom bomb. Re-reading my columns it's clear that they were more thoughtful and eclectic after that moment.

When I found myself in radio in 1981 I was surprised to learn that thoughts I had, as expressed in editorials, were of interest to many people. And as my radio career progressed I sensed that my thoughts were those of a Canadian from British Columbia and that many related to what other Canadians—such as Dalton

Camp—saw as xenophobia. I started writing for the late *Financial Post* in 1983, continuing, with some substantial breaks, until 1998 nearly always expounding on thoughts I had as a Pacific Coaster who was, I often felt, a Canadian by entrapment. Since 1981 I have written up a storm often as a regular columnist (*The Georgia Straight, The Vancouver Courier, The Financial Post*, and *The Province* as a freelancer) and regularly as an editorialist on my own program.

With this late-arriving outpouring of the written word I added two, now three books and a lot of "essays" written only because I wanted to, and from which this book is drawn.

The hardest part of this process was to make some sense of what started out as about seventy essays on everything from fly fishing, to politics, to God. I am grateful to my editor, Carolyn Bateman, who indeed did find some order in the chaos so that the book is divided into three parts, one about my personal experiences, one about the things I feel passionately about, and one on politics. Needless to say, there are many essays that could be placed in all three categories.

I have been very fortunate to have had four major careers, two minor ones, and one part-time one. The latter was as a golf teaching pro at a driving range when I was an articled law student. The two minor ones, as a flunky in Edmonton with Imperial Oil (I soon found out that I was a coast boy through and through) and with Canadian White Pine as a third assistant safety supervisor, lasted only a few months each. I spent three-and-a-half years as an insurance adjuster for Allstate Insurance (known, wryly, as All Heart), nearly sixteen years in law, five years as a cabinet minister in the Bill Bennett government, and now twenty years as a broadcaster. It's been a slice—and, God willing, it's not over yet.

I hope you'll like this book; the best place to keep it I'm sure is in the loo where, especially as the years go by, it takes a bit longer. The essays—too serious a word but I'm stumped for a synonym—each stand on their own.

I know that one is expected to thank one's editor once only lest they get a swelled head, but I must thank Carolyn again if only because she showed so much patience with me in selecting what we now present to you and for graciously conceding to me that the verb "to be" takes the subjective, not the accusative while for my part I acknowledged a very serious "that" and "which" problem.

I hope you enjoy what follows.

Personal

A LATE BLOOMER

If one is going to reflect, I suppose he must reflect upon his own life. And when I look back there are lots of things to reflect upon—some good, many bad. But what I see most of all is a late bloomer. And we late bloomers are not so numerous as all that because most people who don't bloom early, never bloom at all. I don't mean that unkindly—most who live decent and relatively happy lives have much to be thankful for. There's nothing wrong with finding your niche in life and filling it comfortably. And I don't want to give the impression that my own late blooming is anything special. I have just attained a bit of fame in my own backyard and a small amount of notoriety nationally, but I did it relatively late in life. I think there are lots of people who, later on in life, find that they reach the top of their profession and it comes as a bit of a surprise to them and those who know them. However, when that person or their acquaintances look back, there were probably some flashes of brilliance on occasion.

I think the reason those who bloom late do so is an inherent shyness. Now they may not be shy in all things—I certainly wasn't—but they have a lack of self-confidence when it comes to things that seem to matter to society. The converse is also true. There are people who from the outset bubble with self-confidence and reach places of great importance only to prove great inadequacies when they must perform.

I don't know what happened to me. I was always a good student when forced to be such in private school during my middle school years. Yet after Grade 5, when I led the class, I always neatly avoided ever reaching the top. I was always well placed in the class but never again at the top. And I was and remain a paradox. Highly competitive in many things, I seemed to shy away from competitiveness when everything, such as the gold medal, was at stake. I don't know what this means to the psycho-logist—I was and remain a bad sport. When I say that, I don't mean I can't smile and congratulate the winner. It's just that I hate losing yet often don't seem willing to put forth the effort or make the sacrifices necessary to win.

Part, but only part, of this is a difficulty concentrating on one thing to the exclusion of all others. My mind seems to drift, attach itself to something that is not the subject of the moment, then operate sort of in a parallel universe. I suppose what I'm confessing to is a lack of discipline. I'm by nature a daydreamer.

I used to play very low handicap golf, but I was destroyed by my temper. I was a club thrower and indeed a club breaker and I could never break, so to speak, myself of that habit.

When I analyze it, this was a fear not of failure but of public failure. For like all ill-tempered club throwers, I never displayed that nonsense when I was playing alone. And I suppose it was that tendency that kept me from risking public failure for so long. But—and I tell you this because there may, for all I know, be others with this sort of quirky personality out there—I wasn't consistent in this. I took some very big gambles that risked public humiliation. As president of a golf club in the '60s, I staked my very status in the club on a successful attempt to stamp out the racism that had hitherto made the club White Anglo-Saxon only. I made a career move in my late thirties that risked a successful though deadly dull law practice in my home town of Vancouver for a new career in Kamloops where I knew scarcely a soul. Then, a year later, I left the security of the firm I had joined to venture out on my own.

It was here, in a smaller pond, that I became a bigger frog, and two cases in which I was involved got me a lot of public attention, some national media coverage, and a platform from which to launch a political career.

In my first year there I got into a hell of a row with the legal profession that took on national proportions, and it happened like this. I was hired by Legal Aid, at the princely sum of fifty dollars per day, to defend one of three young people charged in a brutal hammer murder. The preliminary hearing lasted some sixteen days, and upon the accuseds' committal for trial I informed the judge that I considered my job finished but that if the attorney-general were to raise my pay to equal that of the prosecutor I would reconsider. All hell broke loose and it became a national story about how this money-grubbing lawyer had abandoned his client. The local bar association met and condemned my actions (four years later I was president of the same Kamloops Bar Association), and letters to the newspapers raged to and fro. One senior lawyer castigated my lack of commitment to the high calling of barrister, to be rebutted by another who pointed out that such criticism was easy from one who never took such cases himself. The Kamloops Bar hadn't seen anything like it in years. Kind of livened the place up, I did.

The issue was a real one. Most lawyers, including me from the start, took their share of Legal Aid, often for free. Most of the time this involved perhaps an hour or two of time on impaired driving cases, or shoplifting offences. And I did these cases cheerfully and to the best of my ability. But this case was a bit much. At those wages I simply couldn't pay my way in my firm.

Eventually the honour of the Kamloops Bar was restored when Russ Chamberlain, then a young criminal lawyer, now a not-so-young but very eminent one, came from Vancouver to save the day. The case had a couple of interesting ramifications. I believe the actions I took did a great deal to make Legal Aid a bit more fair but it led to a curious meeting between me and Peter Millward, later a county court and supreme court judge, who was then the bencher of the Law Society for the county of Yale and thus was "my" bencher. He asked me to drop by his office, which I did.

"Rafe," he said, "it's my unpleasant duty to reprimand you on behalf of the Discipline Committee for your actions in the Hough case."

"Pete," I replied, "it's a funny thing but I don't recall the hearing."

"Now, Rafe," he replied, "that's not the way we do things. No need for hearings. The discipline committee just asked me to convey to you their reprimand. That's how they deal with these matters when they happen 'up country.'"

"You and the benchers can go fuck yourselves, Pete," was my response. "If you have a complaint against my conduct, lay a formal charge and I will answer it. Moreover I'm going to my office now to send a letter, in somewhat less descriptive language, to the treasurer telling him to prosecute or butt out." Millward tried to dissuade me, as did my law partners, but I sent such a letter and made it plain that the very least lawyers should do is give justice to other lawyers and that I wasn't going to be convicted without a hearing.

I heard nothing more on the subject and some months later I saw the treasurer, John Bouck, now and for many years a supreme court judge, and in the course of the conversation I asked him if I could consider the matter closed. He smiled both with his mouth and eyes and said, "You'll not be hearing any more of the matter, and I think my colleagues have abandoned the practice of sending friendly little reprimands to 'up country' lawyers through the local bencher."

The second case was even more attention-grabbing.

There was a cabaret in Kamloops called Friar Tucks run by a larger-than-life lady named Liz Biggar. It was very popular for lunch, especially after Liz hired a bottomless dancer named Linda Adams. Took it all off, she did. And it was not long before she was charged with obscenity by the local fuzz.

I was retained by Friar Tucks and Peter Jensen, a very able criminal lawyer acted for Linda Adams, and an old sailor from the war days, Bill Turlock, prosecuted. I was rather surprised at the vigour Bill brought to the task because he seemed to be a man of the world, but at any rate he took his job very seriously. It was great fun and lasted, as I recall, for about a week.

The entire case hinged on what were the community standards when it came to such things. Turlock wanted Peter and me to admit certain things, which seemed obvious—such as she had indeed exposed her vagina—but, on Peter's advice, we refused.

Turned out he had a reason.

The main RCMP witness couldn't have been more than twenty and if he had ever shaved, the morning of his testimony was the first time. He took the stand and related how he had watched this performance—in the company of some of Kamloops' finest citizens including most of the legal profession—and that after Linda had removed her upper clothing she pulled down her pants and exposed her "gentile" region. It was for me to cross-examine first and I took from my file a copy of *The Happy Hooker*, a lurid and detailed description of the life of a whore by Xaviera Hollander, getting the constable to agree that this book was readily available at Kamloops newsstands. Then, to a packed and tittering audience, I read passages from it including the time she gets screwed by her German Shepherd dog. And on each occasion I asked the poor constable how the behaviour described by Ms. Hollander compared to the simple act by Ms. Adams of taking her pants off. But it was Peter Jensen who stole the show. After getting the blushing constable to describe Ms. Adams' crotch in as much detail as possible, Jensen pulled from his file a G-string covered in hair. This, said Jensen, was a vaginal hairpiece and could the constable be certain that it wasn't something like this she had been wearing?

It was pandemonium shared, I might say, by the late Stuart Van Male, the judge who, like most sensible people, thought the entire matter was an enormous waste of public time and money. But Turlock and the Crown pressed on. Then it was our turn. We called as a witness John Pifer, columnist and broadcaster, then as now a Renaissance man who would be the last person on earth to find anything like this remotely obscene. As would be expected, he thought the only thing wrong with Linda Adams' performance was that she couldn't dance worth a damn. Then from somewhere we produced a rather odd lady whom we somehow qualified as an expert on dancing, who gave as evidence that the only lewd dancing was ballroom dancing since that was the only kind where the partners touched each other.

The case ended after Judge Van Male decided to "take a view," so we all hustled down to Friar Tucks where Linda showed the judge, in all its naked wonder, the beauty of her performance.

It so happened that there was a case from the Appellate Division of the Alberta Supreme Court before the Supreme Court of Canada on all fours, so to speak, with the Adams' case, so Peter and I asked Judge Van Male to postpone his decision for a time until we could hear what the top court in the land had to say. He agreed.

Finally, after several weeks of postponement, Van Male could wait no longer. It turned out that he had a speech on this subject he had to unburden himself of so away he went. He went up one side of the prosecution and down the other and in a brilliantly witty as well as wise judgement found Linda Adams guilty and fined her one dollar!

But that was not the end of the story. Peter and I promptly appealed! For all its "show-biz quality," there was a principle here. And in a few weeks the Supreme Court of Canada ruled, in effect, in Linda's favour. Appeals from provincial court in those days went by way of a complete re-hearing before a county court judge. As I recall it, Pat Dohm, now a Supreme Court judge and deputy chief justice, took the appeal for the crown, simply called no evidence and the acquittal was registered. The only thing remaining was who was to gain possession of the cheque for one dollar returned after the acquittal and I lost the toss.

If these trials did nothing else, they made me well known in my adoptive city and came at a time when I was seriously thinking about what I was going to do with my life. In a way I was a victim of my own deep-seated prejudices. I was part of "old

Vancouver," yet I rebelled against what I had been born to. I refused to article with the law firms that my father had close friends in but went instead to a rebel who constantly took on the established law firms. I had a very strong desire to make my own way and in a sense that prevented me from using stepping stones that were there for me if I wished. Undoubtedly there were plenty of gremlins at work deep inside my psyche because when I did start to bloom, at about age forty, it was because I had made a fresh start in the relatively smaller centre of Kamloops in which I wasn't known. When I look back on it, it all happened so quickly.

Four years after arriving in Kamloops I successfully ran as alderman and two years later was their member of the Legislative Assembly and a cabinet minister. From the start of my political career, I felt as if I had been reborn. I knew I wanted to accomplish things in government and I can unblushingly say that I did. I was a very active consumer minister who brought in landmark legislation all of which remains on the books. I had a fine time as minister responsible for constitutional affairs, trusted by the premier implicitly to represent British Columbia's views, and I had a spell as environment minister and health minister. By the time I was forty-nine, I had quite a respectable curriculum vitae.

For a man who had had such problems with self-confidence in the past, I upped stakes and left government in early 1981 to become a broadcaster in public affairs, hosting my own show without having had any experience whatsoever. In the days when this was a hell of a lot of money, I demanded and received a three-year contract at $100,000 per year at a top station doing their number-one show without any idea of what I was doing.

And I started to write for, really, the first time unless you count the MLA columns I used to do for the papers back in the constituency. By 1983 I was writing for the *Financial Post*, a column I wrote intermittently for fifteen years. I was offered columns, which I turned down, in the *Globe and Mail* (because I dislike the paper intensely), and the *Vancouver Sun* (because I smelled a rat and thought they simply wanted to take me away from the *Vancouver Courier* for whom I was writing, then dump me). By the time I was sixty I had the most-listened-to show in Western Canada and perhaps the entire country (with the exception of Peter Gzowski who was cross Canada—I slaughtered him in the local ratings) and was seen and heard as a political commentator across the country. I have now, with this, written three books—all since turning forty.

It's fascinating to look back from the vantage point of my late sixties and see what a change came in my mid-forties. I'm not sure I know quite what hit me. It was a horrible time in many ways. My lovely daughter Shawn was killed in a car crash in October 1976, which, no doubt in my mind, spawned a broken marriage and a disastrous re-marriage. For the entire year of 1977, mourning my daughter and badly hurting my wife, Eve, I was in a daze. The record shows that it was a very productive year in terms of legislation and development of government policy, but to me it's all enveloped in a hazy half memory. But for all that there's no doubt that my life can be easily divided into two parts—the first forty years or so, the years the locusts ate, and from then until now a frenetic drive to catch up.

Why did this all happen?

I think it was because when I turned forty, or thereabouts, I felt that I had wasted my life. I had played too much golf (by far), drunk too much whiskey and played too much cards (ditto), and chased too many women (ditto again). I looked back and saw a barren stretch with tiny little occasional oases of accomplishment and was scared that I'd blown it. I became, in a sense, possessed by the thought that if I didn't get off my ass I would have pissed away my life.

Why am I telling you all this?

First, because I think any reader has the right to know something about the author. Second, because I sense there may be others out there who think that because they haven't accomplished what they wanted by a certain age they are doomed to miss the boat.

I have not really accomplished all that much. But I have, in the past twenty-five years, attained more of my potential than before. And that surely is what it's all about. Not very many of us will go right to the top, but we can do better—and if one is a late bloomer, it might help to know that you can do better even with a self-imposed slow start.

OUT OF THE SHADOWS

This is a personal story of mental illness—and it's a mental illness suffered by one in five Canadians. Women have a higher rate of depression, but many men are reluctant to admit to the condition. And that's a very large part of the problem.

I am clinically depressed and have been for more than ten years. I think it a fair assumption that everyone knows someone with clinical depression, often someone within their immediate family.

What exactly is depression? I am not a doctor and do not intend to come close to a medical explanation here. I content myself with my own definition, which is simple: "An ongoing inability to cope." It takes many forms and is often part of, or at least associated with, more serious mental illness, such as schizophrenia. In my case, it means uncontrollable anxiety.

What we're talking about isn't the routine sort of depression that accompanies the everyday hard knocks of life, such as the loss of a job or the death of a loved one. I happen to believe that these natural unhappy events can, through a sort of "piling on" process, either lead to or aggravate clinical depression, but they are not that in themselves.

Clinical depression is a chronic ailment that requires ongoing treatment. Often a psychiatrist's help will be needed (I've seen two) to confirm the diagnosis and work out the appropriate medication, but in the vast majority of cases, clinical depression can be treated by medicine prescribed by a family doctor.

I've told my story in my book *Canada: Is Anyone Listening?* but here's a shortened version in the hopes that someone reading it may see something familiar and get help. Depression is not something to be ashamed of, because it is not a character flaw.

Like everyone else, I've borne my share of life's problems. In my case they included the sudden death of a teenage daughter, a consequent divorce because of my inability to deal with that tragedy, serious financial problems, and highly stressful occupations. (I've been a lawyer, cabinet minister, and broadcaster.)

I woke up one day in March 1988 with a pain in my right side that threw me into a panic. I had never experienced this sort of sustained panic before and I concluded that I must be dying of liver cancer, a diagnosis I quickly confirmed by looking under L in the *Columbia Medical Encyclopedia*.

Even after seeing my doctor, having ultrasound tests, and getting the firm diagnosis that I had gallstones, I remained utterly convinced that I was dying of liver cancer and that the doctors were lying to me. It's hard to explain how this deep anxiety works, but it was devastating. There was an overwhelming feeling of doom, and none of my defences, the ones we all erect around ourselves, could keep it out.

As it happened, I was lucky. My doctor was one of a very few general practitioners at that time who both understood depression and recognized its signs. While I was berating him for not telling the truth about my cancer, he asked how long ago it was that my daughter had been killed.

Within minutes and about five questions later, I was in a flood of tears. I was, the doctor told me, clinically depressed, and my form of depression was anxiety. But there was help.

I was reluctant to accept this at first. After all, men of sturdy stock didn't have this sort of problem, did we? Our tradition was stiff upper lip, Sir Francis Drake, British pluck, Land of Hope and Glory, and all that. I soon learned a new word: serotonin. The absence or shortage of this chemical causes depression. Depression is really no different from diabetes (I have that too) in that the body doesn't adequately supply a necessary chemical.

Happily, I learned, serotonin substitutes are readily available, the most prominent of which is Prozac. My doctor prescribed an anti-anxiety medicine called Elavil Plus that was particularly effective for my form of depression, which is quite common.

Within a couple of weeks I felt better than I ever had in my life. For the next nine years, apart from the daily reminder when I took the medicine, I gave no thought to depression. Then I made the serious mistake of trying to fix something that wasn't broken. I interviewed a prominent American psychiatrist one day, and he spoke of a new medicine called Serzone that was all the rage. I got the impression that I was using the tin Lizzie of antidepressants and that I ought to buy the latest model. Because I had a mildly unpleasant side effect (all depression medications can have side effects), I broached the subject of changing medicines with my doctor. He wasn't thrilled with the idea but nevertheless prescribed Serzone for me, and I switched. It was a serious mistake. I had to withdraw from all medicine for two weeks and only gradually increase the dose of the new one. I went through utter hell, and by the time I was used to the new medicine I discovered that it too can have side effects. I suffered a morning hangover that reminded me of college days after a fraternity bash. Since a couple of cans of light beer are now a big night for me, not only did I hate the hangover but I felt cheated of the party. Ten months later I changed back to Elavil Plus and all's well.

I have done radio shows with specialists on depression, so I know that not only am I not a rare case but depression in Canadian society is widespread and devastating. It by no means always takes the same form as mine, but it is there.

It's there in all manner of anti-social behaviour. It's there in the valued employee who suddenly seems to have lost his stuff or the employee of real promise who somehow can't keep up with the changes taking place. It's even there with kids, and most tragically with those who kill themselves.

I now look back at a father who drank too much and see a

man—a wonderful, loving man—who couldn't cope and used the only medicine then available to him, whiskey. I look back at a nephew by marriage who killed himself at fifteen and see a youngster who needed help that wasn't there. Mainly, though, I look back at myself and see how lucky I was to have a doctor who understood depression.

Here's what this depressed person did last year: I hosted five two-and-a-half-hour radio shows a week with a prepared editorial each day, wrote three newspaper articles every week, did numerous speaking engagements and guest appearances on radio and TV—and wrote a book.

When I was growing up during the Second World War, mental illness was not a subject that could be discussed. I come from traditional British stock—one grandmother was born in Salisbury, England, the other on Cape Breton Island. One grandfather was born of English parents in Minneapolis and the other in Auckland, New Zealand. In our world, boys didn't cry. It was a masculine world where the heroes were Cecil Rhodes and, of course, Sir Winston Churchill, my lifelong hero.

In those days, people were divided into the sane and the insane. The latter, if untreatable or dangerous, were sent to an asylum, often for life. The depressed, more often than not with drinking problems, were just explained away.

We like to think we've made great advances in the field of mental health, and I suppose that if you don't measure that progress against too strict a standard, we have. But we have a long way to go.

We still talk about "mental health" and have Mental Health Acts throughout the country. Why do we make this distinction? Isn't "health" just health? If not, why not? Because we're frightened stiff of mental illness, or we joke about it. A disc jockey at the radio station I work for once commented that his school was so small that the debating team was one schizophrenic.

Society indulges in a sort of gallows humour to cover up its collective insecurity about mental illness. We're not only afraid of what mentally ill people might do to our loved ones or us, we fear that we ourselves might be so afflicted. The stigma attached to mental illness is still, by far, the biggest barrier to its cure. Because sufferers fear the societal consequences of being diagnosed as depressed, they suffer the even greater consequences of remaining untreated.

Oh yes, about that reference to Winston Churchill—politician, soldier, statesman, journalist, Nobel laureate for literature, painter, and saviour of the Western world—he suffered from depression all of his adult life.

THERE HAVE BEEN
A FEW CHANGES

I was born and raised in Vancouver, and I'm here to tell you there have been some changes! In Vancouver, in British Columbia, and across the entire country.

Other than the climate and the glorious scenery, I don't suppose Vancouver was much different than most Canadian cities outside Quebec when I was born on New Years' Eve, 1931. We were all sort of British—maybe in some ways more British than the British themselves. We sang "God Save the King" a lot, and whenever it came on the radio at home we were all expected to stand up. It was played after every movie of course. We sang the "Maple Leaf Forever" with its astonishing bigotry and the version of "O Canada" in which we vowed to be "At Britain's side, whate'er betide." Everyone knew the words to "Rule Britannia" and "The British Grenadiers," and "The Londonderry Air" was the melody of a hymn called "My Own Dear Land." You would have thought all of us lived in the Cotswolds.

Most of our radio was American, however. The CBC was there for CBC types, who haven't changed much over the years, but if you wanted to hear Jack Armstrong, the All-American Boy, or Terry and the Pirates, it was KOMO 710AM Seattle you tuned into.

Downtown Vancouver was dominated by the Vancouver Hotel as Toronto used to be by the Royal York Hotel—both are dwarfed in their respective skylines now by the steel and mostly glass edifices that abound. And a big treat for us kids was to "dine in the sky" at the Sylvia Hotel on English Bay, the "sky" being the eighth floor!

Vancouver was a superb place to grow up. In Kerrisdale, where I lived until aged sixteen, we had several acres of woods behind our house and a dairy farm up the street. The North Shore rivers such as the Capilano, the Lynn, and the Seymour were wonderful sources of adventure, and the pools we used to dive into from the cliffs above are closed now for that sort of dangerous behaviour.

But the Vancouver of my youth was the era where the "good people" were Anglicans and United Church folks, and we weren't all that sure about the latter. Catholics and Protestants rarely intermarried, and if they did, Archbishop Duke made sure the ceremony wasn't in the main church in front of the altar but in a chapel in the rear, and that the kids were brought up Catholic. "Lesser breeds," including Jews, lived in different parts of town than the rest of us. "Chinamen" drove vegetable trucks, took our laundry, and, so we supposed, spent the rest of their time in opium dens. "Japs" fished, farmed, and looked after our gardens. "Hunkies," as Ukrainians were called, farmed and were on occasion graciously permitted to play for the Toronto Maple Leafs to show how tolerant and liberal Conn Smythe's team was. It did not, it must be noted however, go so far as to permit French-Canadians to play. The hierarchy was set in stone. Lesser breeds didn't vote or belong to professions—they were expected to know their place. When Doug Jung, two years my senior in law school and the first Canadian lawyer of Chinese descent, had the temerity to contest Vancouver Centre and win for the Tories, the old, so-established Liberal senator J. W. deB. Farris was apoplectic and could only sputter "that Chinaman."

Women knew their place then too—it was in the home cooking, sewing, and making babies. And if the old man belted her about a bit from time to time, the police would seldom even answer the call, it being only a domestic affair. The hubby could get drunk, screw around to his heart's content, and slap the little woman around and nothing was said. She just smiled and knew her place, which, to the limited extent it was outside the home, was at church or working for the "Thrift Shop." Divorce was virtually impossible for most women both for social and financial reasons, and we kidded ourselves that it was because "ladies" really liked their spot in the social pyramid.

Indians, of course, were not even people. They were whatever the Indian Act from time to time said they were. Our society gave them a massive alcohol problem then complained that they were mostly drunks.

The only real citizens were those of British extraction. Every once in a while a Polish name like Gzowski popped up in faraway places like Toronto, but that just served as a bit of seasoning to the Anglo-Saxon mix. And as for Jews, it was like my Dad said—while there is the occasional good Jew, they're "kikes," not to be trusted, and for God's sake don't let one in your club because the next thing you know you'll be swamped with them.

Of course lawyers did more gentlemanly things back then, but some lawyers—personal injury lawyers like my very good friend and teacher Tommy Griffiths—were looked upon as uncouth mouthpieces because they used juries to separate flint-hearted but oh-so-proper Toronto insurance companies from their spoils. In those days there were no lawyers standing up for people's rights because the people who needed those rights, the Chinese, the Japanese, what we called Hindus back then, the Indians, and of course women, were prevented by the social structure in which they were stuck from making a fuss.

Like other anglophone Canadian cities, the Vancouver I grew up in was run by family compacts—all nice and white and mostly Anglo-Saxon. For those in the upper third of that pyramid, things were terrific. When you graduated from university, your Dad always knew someone. And you continued as part of the great Canadian Oligarchy as your parents and grandparents had done before you.

Those were the days when we in that oligarchy should have remembered the words of John Donne, for they were to prove so apt: "Never send to ask for whom the bell tolls; it tolls for thee."

And it started to toll, slowly at first after the war, then more and more quickly, and it still does for me and mine. It tolls to tell us that Canada's not a white Anglo-Saxon country with a bunch of rather tiresome French-Canadians thrown in any more—indeed it hasn't been that from the outset. Minorities—and women—began to believe us when we talked about democracy, freedom, tolerance, civility, and a fair chance for all, and they stepped up to take their turn at bats.

The feminist movement came to Vancouver, as it did everywhere. Immigration, whether we liked it or not—and many didn't and don't—came in a big way, and we were forced to live either in harmony or at each other's throats. For the most part, we chose the former. This has raised the cry from many WASP Canadians that newcomers are not adapting to and accepting Canadian culture. But culture is always a moving thing unless you live in a place like Iceland, and even there I'm sure that the Information Age makes older folks uncomfortable. In Canada there is not one culture but dozens that play with and against one another. It's rather like kids' Plasticine or Silly Putty. You can mix the colours together and make one cohesive ball, but you'll still be able to see the individual colours. Just as the English language that absorbs rather than rejects new words has profited immensely by doing so, so will Vancouver, British Columbia, and the country prosper by accepting, as its own, the contributions of all who come here as additions to, not subtractions from, its essence.

Political and other institutions have reflected and continue to reflect these changes. Accompanied by great resentment in many parts of B.C., especially behind the "Tweed Curtain" in Victoria, there was much indignation in the late '70s when the provincial government made Canadian citizenship a prerequisite to voting. Until then if one was British, well, what more did one need? This event, which affected so few, was a very big sign that the oligarchy was crumbling if it hadn't already crumbled. Of course there have been troubles. There is resentment and there is bigotry. But surprisingly little. As I write this three Indo-Canadians sit in the B.C. Legislature, two in cabinet, and one of them as premier.

My hometown and native province have changed, and they will never be the same again. And what does this old Vancouverite think of all this? Marvellous. Bloody marvellous. The city is the most wonderful, cosmopolitan place in the world.

New citizens have brought new colour—and food. The eating out in Vancouver is not only fantastic for a city this size, I believe that in Canada only Montreal can come close. Every neighbourhood has its ethnic restaurants and they're mostly very good. Most of all it's the feel of the place. It feels mature—still some rough edges caused by older people who have difficulty adapting—but mature. It's a grown-up city. In fact, it really grew up without any "teen" years, and that may account for what problems we do occasionally have.

The things wrong with my Vancouver are the same things that are wrong with any small city that becomes a big one rather quickly. I wish we still had the streetcars and could leave our cars unlocked and the doors of our homes open. But so does everyone else who lives in the modern city. Still, I'm a better person I think—all of us are better people—for having to learn tolerance and, more than that, for having to learn something about other people, different people. And they are better too. The kids of all communities especially are better for it.

What was could not remain. It often seems so good in retrospect, but so does everything. In fact, it's better now. By far. Vancouver, the place of my birth and my residence for most of my life, is a hell of a good place to live and, I suspect, so say most if not all of us.

GOD AND THE GOLF BALL

Traditionally at Easter I review with my listeners how I'm doing with the Christianity bit. In doing so I usually manage to make almost everyone who reads me or listens to me angry. Many Protestants write me with solemn intonations quoting various parts of the Bible to show how my evil thoughts are condemning me and all who listen to eternal perdition. Roman Catholics who have never forgiven Henry VIII much less Martin Luther generally rebuke me but in kindly fashion, while the atheists and agnostics are even more convinced I've gone mad.

Over the past five years or so I've not been fighting with other Christians or indeed with followers of other faiths. No, I've been battling the forces of science, which insist they have the answers. Although world science hasn't heard about it yet, I demolished them in an Easter dissertation, which I then fortified the following year.

You may remember when leading scientists declared that not only was the universe created by a big bang but that it started with an object about the size of a golf ball. Now I've been gentler in my criticisms of science and its rather arrogant assumption than science has been to Christians. Science mocks Christ's miracles and his resurrection as being mumbo-jumbo, yet I held my tongue. I didn't mock *them* for what most of us lesser folks would see as sheer idiocy. How the devil could the universe begin from matter the size of a golf ball? And if there was a big bang, what was it that banged? Nothingness? An exploding void?

No, what I said is simply this—science and religion have now reached the same cavern of the unknown. For while science asks me, "If there's a God, who made God?" I with Jesuitical cleverness answer with a question, "Well, then if not God, who made that golf ball?"

This past year I started to think along the lines of a court trial. If neither science nor religion can, short of simple faith, answer their respective questions, what was the evidence? At least what was the evidence for religion? (The scientists can hire their own counsel.)

In fact, they have. This is what Bertrand Russell stated in 1961: "...Man is the product of causes which had no provision for the end they were achieving; that his origin, his growth, his hopes and fears, his loves and his beliefs, are but the outcome of accidental collocation of atoms; that no fire, no heroism, no intensity of thought and feeling, can preserve an individual life beyond the grave; that all the labours of the ages, all the devotions, all the inspiration, all the noonday brightness of human genius, are destined to extinction in the vast death of the solar system, and that the whole temple of Man's achievement must be inevitably buried beneath the debris of a universe in ruins—all these things, if not quite beyond dispute, are yet so nearly certain, that no philosophy which rejects them can hope to stand."

That's their case; here is mine.

A lot of things came to my mind and have not as yet, I freely confess, been marshalled into a final brief.

There is life itself. And there is the life of a human being with millions of living organisms in or on that human body, feasting away to their hearts' content, all in balance. And there's all the other life on the planet, so perfectly in balance in convenient and well-established food chains (until humans mess with the system). Science tells us that the billions of creatures on this planet all simply started with "life" (with no good explanation as to how that happened) and the rest is just evolution.

I say, perhaps, but what was it that guided that evolution? How did that precious thing known as life begin? Can we simply say that all the plants and animals mysteriously adjusted to their particular environment because of Mother Nature, namely evolution? What makes this evolution work? Just who is this "Mother Nature"? Surely science, when it talks this way, is covering up its gigantic ignorance with a pat word—evolution.

And I thought of how life sustains itself in a giant ecosystem, which contains within it hundreds of millions, nay, billions, of sub-ecosystems. This, science teaches us, is again evolution—the mere chance resulting from billions of chance events and things converging into one scientific miracle. "Mother Nature" is such a great phrase because it shuts down so many arguments, but I ask myself, "What does that phrase mean?" When I am asked to have faith in evolution and Mother Nature, is that so much different than being asked to believe about a Man of miracles?

And as I thought this through and threw facts together for my brief, my pleadings as it were, one argument came to me that I'm content to put out as my only argument against the golf ball people—it's a four-letter word.

L-O-V-E. Plain ordinary love. Where does that come from?

Love. Explain that one to me, Mr., Ms, or I suppose it's Dr. Scientist. What happens on that first day of kindergarten when you take a shine to that little girl in the front row, so much so that you deny to all that you even like her? What happens when, in later life, you really do fall in love, not just lust, which hits us all at hopping hormone time? I mean when you reach the stage that you simply want one person for your own for all time. Is it just a visual thing?

Of course not, for blind people fall in love like everyone else does. Then is it a verbal thing? No, for deaf people fall in love too. Is it just a sexual thing? Of course not, otherwise we older, slightly heavier, distinctly unsexy people would be lonely. And not very many people in this world are what we would call beautiful yet most of us love and are loved. We also know that people can fall in love by letter or even on the Internet.

And what about the fondness we feel for friends? We all have best friends, and there is certainly no sexuality about it and sometimes our best friends come into our lives later in life.

Is love just the reverse side of the coin with hate on it? It would certainly seem so given the way some relationships end, but even then there's a capacity for some vestige of love as time passes and it takes the form of forgiveness.

And then there is the love of parents for children and vice versa. This isn't always there, of course, and it's a great pity when it isn't. But it's a love and a very strong love. There is an even more difficult form of love to explain—that, for example, of a Mother Theresa. Or the love that gets us all opening our hearts, and wallets, for people we have never seen yet for whose suffering we feel great empathy. For some the suffering of faraway peoples means but a mild and short-lived financial sacrifice, but what of those who run soup kitchens, help those who are diseased, or work for good in places that are highly dangerous?

What all types of love have in common is that there is no explanation. We speak of chemistry where none can be demonstrated. A person falls in love with one identical twin yet not with the other. We know that love is there, but we can't see it or touch it. We look for deep psychological reasons for things to be as they are and come up empty.

Yet all of us have relationships. Some are a sort of teamwork as in partners at golf or tennis that just seem to work out well. Some of them are founded on an ability to integrate differing strengths. Some of them are comfortable, more than anything else. Many, indeed most relationships have a great many factors and they may not be the same for both sides.

Scientists, when faced with describing the feelings that make up relationships, usually mumble something about instinct or nature's way, which is no better mumbo-jumbo than that chanted by an ancient priest to a volcano. We cannot answer what love is just as we cannot answer the question, "If there's a God, who made God?"

The answer to both questions is beyond our human capacity to understand. God is…Love is…they're probably the same thing, and to know that is to know all you need to know.

It can't be explained away by that old Mother Nature bit—we must propagate our kind so this is nature's way, blah, blah, blah. Indeed it can't be explained away just by sexual attraction, though I challenge the golf ball crowd to explain how *that* works in precise, scientific terms. The orgasm itself may be the biggest miracle of all next to love. No, love is the great mystery, which, when all is said and done, is the challenge to science.

To paraphrase the great American comedian, Will Rogers, I am a member of no organized religion—I'm an Anglican. But over the past five or six years that I've been debating these issues—often with my wife but mostly with myself—I've become satisfied that the word of Christ is for real. And in saying that, I heartily and happily concede that the words of other holy people are for real too, and that their adherents are God's children like the rest of us. I still have, and no doubt always will have, problems with some tenets of belief, but I have read the New Testament and have come to believe that Jesus wasn't much for nitpicking. He performed miracles on the Sabbath and kept his nose out of politics. He was all about a standard of conduct that is the hallmark of all great religions—you shall love God and your neighbour. The operative word throughout the teachings of Christ is love—a state of affairs beyond the abilities of any scientist to explain in concrete scientific terms.

Given that science is, clutching its golf ball, standing at the same cavern I am, unable to prove anything beyond a shadow of a doubt, I say my case is proved beyond all reasonable doubt.

In short, I rest my case.

GROWING OLD

I n addition to being frightening as hell, growing old is an
experience you don't know is happening until it's happened.
Perhaps that's why it's so frightening. You wake up one morning
wondering where the last decade suddenly went to. It occurs to
you that while you never used to, you read the obituary page
every day. And funerals are no longer a once a year affair.

But the good news is that however much you may, suddenly,
see yourself as having become old, you reject the notion. That's
because these days a person doesn't have the finish line his parents did. We don't die suddenly of a heart attack at forty-five—
or suffer a stroke at fifty. Some of us do, of course, but even then
we're far more likely to survive than our parents were. These
days the old retiring age of sixty-five means very little to most
who, if they are forced out of a job by age, simply find another
one, perhaps run out of their own home. From the old statis-
tical lists of birth, marriage, divorce, retirement, and death we
probably must subtract the "retirement" category because it is
now incapable of any precise definition. This means that where
once the line of demarcation between middle age and old age
was sixty-five and the mandatory gold watch, now the realiza-
tion of old age comes in various and often shocking ways. These
are likely to be an accumulation of events that may or may not
come after one's sixty-fifth birthday.

The later retirement, if it comes at all, has I think two
causes. First of all, we're much healthier than our parents were.
We don't smoke, for one thing, and not only does that account
for how much younger we look, it means that we play tougher

games like squash much longer, which connects us in real ways to the next generation. In my parents' day, people at sixty-five looked and acted like old people because physically they were. But mentally they were old too because they had nothing to look forward to each day except those things a senior was expected to do. So retirement, that perennial symbol of old age, is not happening—at least not as soon.

But there is another reason for this. We no longer have that game plan of life laid out for us—into the bank as a clerk, a steady move up through the corporate game of snakes and ladder, eye always on that magic date of retirement. Today's person will have several jobs, indeed several careers. And because the lifespan of each of these careers is so short, why not take another one on in your sixties instead of retiring? After all, the commitment needn't be a long one.

The computer is keeping us young as more and more seniors get online. One of my best friends, finally forced into retirement at eighty from the real estate business near Auckland, New Zealand, bought a computer, was mesmerized by the Internet, and is now looking for ways to launch yet another career. He has become an international correspondent and now is almost as close to his sons in Ontario and his pal in Vancouver as if he were actually with them.

Having said all those things, there comes a day that you are old—no doubt a much fitter old than your parents were and probably with more years to come than they had. But you're still old and it's often the milestones that get you.

Your oldest child turns forty—that's a dandy. And if it's three out of four with one thirty-nine, as in my case, it can be a bit overwhelming. Actually my eldest grandson turning twenty was the hardest blow to absorb. Can I be all that far from great-grandfatherhood? Gadfrey Daniel!

And things suddenly hit you. In your club, instead of older men coming up to you saying "I knew your father," young men come to you and say "I know your son" or, even worse, "I know your grandson, went to school with him." Out of the blue your club dues are reduced or even eliminated and you mutter, "But that's only for old farts." The ticket taker at the ferry terminal no longer asks to see your Gold Card so you can get on for free. "C'mon," you wheeze under your breath. "Make my day. Demand proof of my age, dammit!" But it isn't happening any more.

You find yourself fishing a little closer to your car than you once did and now, after falling in three times the year before, you use a wading staff. Your squash partner has stopped calling, and you don't press the matter, And you're quite prepared to walk up to that lovely female pharmacist and present your prescription for Viagra.

Then there are the funerals. The ubiquitous funerals. Every morning you scan the Births and Deaths column praying that there aren't more "sixty-seven-is-too-young-to-die" folks listed. Your weekly planner must become more flexible to accommodate that one-more-time-this-month singing of "Abide with Me" over the bier of another old pal.

There is—at least in my case—a strong sense of urgency and a bemoaning of all the time wasted drinking, gambling, playing golf, and chasing women. Why didn't I read more? Write things that were in my mind instead of using them as an argument after a boozy night at the local watering hole? And why didn't I save some money? But the urgency is not so much over regrets for the past—it makes pretty pleasant thinking sometimes, especially as I try to go to sleep—but about getting things done I want left behind me.

I write more, think more, argue more, and rebel against authority more. I lose patience more and, when asked to do something I don't want to do—like sitting through four hours of opera—ask aloud: "Why the hell should I waste four hours of my ever-diminishing life span on that crap?!"

You may—I have—find yourself returning to church and approaching the questions you once had with urgency instead of skepticism. God, death, the hereafter, and your lifetime batting average in the "being good" department take on new importance. I have found, as a person born to Christianity, a strong desire to prioritize the beliefs I'm expected to have. Thinking that hypocrisy will count against me even more than heresy, I've found myself telling God that I believe the essentials, truly believe them, but I hope he'll forgive me if I express to him my doubts on such matters as the physical resurrection of Christ in exchange for profoundly believing in his teachings about loving God, one's neighbour, and oneself.

I find that old age has brought new vigour to my life—and in that I know I differ from most in my father's generation. Of course I find myself using the health care system more, but I'm also looking at ways to prevent problems. I eat much better and I exercise regularly. I have also discovered a little trick that makes the passing years much more tolerable—I worry about things that are going to happen long after I'm gone. When I say "worry" I suppose I mean that I'm concerned to the point that I place myself in the shoes of my grandchildren and try to figure life from their angle. If I, barely a year from it, begin to see life in terms of the Biblical lifespan, I'll simply become grumpier and grumpier the closer I get. But keeping my mind young, I keep the rest of me young as well.

This attitude would have been much harder for my Dad's generation. For one thing, his life had a "set piece" ambience about it. He wasn't expected to do anything after he reached a certain age, and if he didn't accept that, there wasn't much he could do about it unless he wanted to become a security guard in a rest home until he occupied one of the beds himself. With the advances in medical science and indeed in the alternative health field, I and my generation not only have a longer lifespan than our parents had, we're probably ten years younger at sixty-five than they were at the same age. Moreover, there is so much information out there now and so many ways to convert it both to money and pleasure that it takes a conscious effort to stop yourself and quit the mainstream world just because you've hit a certain anniversary.

All in all, as the man says, old age ain't all that bad when you consider the alternative, which is no longer just death but lots more things to do and much more time to do them.

To adapt a saying of Dr. Johnson's to this context—a sixty-fifth birthday, like a hanging in a fortnight, concentrates the mind wonderfully. However, the focus of that attention, unlike during Dr. Johnson's time, can be more on the years of productive and fun things to do.

THE CORPORATE CHURCH

L ike most born to the church, I strayed after my late teens.
Until then I was sustained by the fact that a lot of pretty
girls—and the occasional very horny one—went to St. John's
Church (Shaughnessy) in Vancouver on Sunday evenings. This
added a new dimension to the weekend for which I was etern-
ally grateful, and I was a pretty regular attender, unless, of
course, the object of my intended ravishing could not for some
reason make it. In any event, by the time I was in my twenties
I had ceased going to church altogether but I hadn't stopped
worrying about those things, such as death, which make churches seem attractive to so many.

Of course I still used the church for things like getting married—I became rather a regular attender for those purposes—
and for funerals such as when my daughter Shawn was killed and
when my parents died. I celebrated Christmas and became very
sentimental at the sight of a well-laid-out nativity scene and very
vocally involved when I could show off my Latin with a rousing
if somewhat unmelodic version of "Adeste Fideles." Only the
first of my four children was christened, as we called it then in
preference to baptism, and none of them attended Sunday
School, which they and I now very much regret.

When I wasn't going to church, I had very good reasons, of
course. My church, I said, was the great outdoors if it was
fishing season although I'm not quite sure what it was when it
wasn't. When I got into philosophical arguments on the subject,
I consistently made the point that the church had done so many
terrible things over the centuries that no decent person should

darken the door of such establishments. My own church had been founded because a reckless and cruel king wanted an annulment so he could marry the young woman he had knocked up. Popes had been rotten. Protestant churches were often cold, humourless places dedicated to making sure no one ever, under any circumstances, had any fun. It didn't seem to me, a lawyer, that the church, any church, could make much of a case.

There endured always, of course, a pull to the habit of my youth. This gave me another excuse not to go to church when the Church of England changed its liturgy from the Book of Common Prayer to the modern stuff. How dare they! After all, on the rare occasions I attended church I rather enjoyed being reminded that I was a miserable sinner and that there was no health in me. The new stuff was not for me. It never occurred to me to me that since I was not a regular communicant I really ought not to have any opinion at all on the subject.

I had always been drawn, rather like a moth to the lamp, to the Catholic Church. It was so old…and so mysterious. And it had such a hold on its devout. The chants in Latin intrigued me, as did their catechism, which could hold, against all common sense and reason, that the wine and bread of communion actually became the blood and body of Christ on consumption. I had always thought that if I ever did return to Christianity it would be as a convert to the Roman Catholic Church.

But such was not to be. I came back to church because the Venerable Louis Rivers (who is very young to be venerable) agreed to marry Wendy and me in 1993, she having been married once before, I twice. His church, St. Christopher's in West Vancouver, is not the nearest Anglican church to where we live but it's less than fifteen minutes away, and after we were married, Wendy and I started attending.

Suddenly, after some months, we quit. Neither of us felt comfortable with the Apostles' Creed, which sets out the critical tenets of the Christian catechism, and I had serious misgivings about the physical ascension of Christ. We stayed away for almost a year. During that time we debated our positions, but neither of us could reconcile ourselves to solemnly plighting our oath to something about which we had doubts.

Just as suddenly, we decided to give it one more try. We had each, quite separately, come to the conclusion that perhaps the catechism, as laid down 1,400 years ago at the Council of Nicea by the Church "establishment" of the day, was not as important as Christ's message, which we deduced was two-fold—actually three-fold when you think of it. We were to love God and love our neighbours as ourselves. Three objects of love: God, our neighbours, ourselves. Not easy laws to live by but very easy to understand.

Having got that far, we rationalized. If Jesus said that His was the path to redemption and if He had laid down these three laws, was it critical that we believed the extra stuff, which might just have been thrown in there by early hustlers of Christianity, of which Saint Paul was rightly the best known? Is it not just possible that, like modern-day advertisers, there was a need back then to package this Jewish religion and make it more saleable to the non-Jews to whom it was being peddled? And that then, as now, mumbo-jumbo was part of the flack's pitch?

Serendipitously, our arrival back at church coincided with a couple of Lou's sermons on the "corporate church" as opposed to God's church. Frankly, I had never thought of it that way, but it made so much sense. Of course there was "the" church, that one founded by Jesus Christ, and there was the "corporate" church as run and so often manipulated by man. God wasn't responsible for the slaughters of the Crusades, or the Inquisition, or the burnings at the stake. It wasn't He who wanted people slaughtered over the question of transubstantiation—whether the host actually became Christ's body and blood. That was man. That was man unredeemed. Of course! God's church was what we aspired to and the corporate church was sort of the clubhouse, with each clubhouse having its own rules.

Now in case he reads this, I would not want my good friend

Lou to feel responsible for however much my beliefs are heretical, but it was his talk about the corporate church that made me content to return to my religious roots.

I must close with this. I have never denied and don't deny today the catechism, the literal words of the creed. If there is a God—and I profoundly believe there is—virgin births and physical ascensions would be mere child's play as would be all the miracles reported in the Bible. I have just come to believe that absolute acceptance of such matters are not critical to being a Christian. The only thing critical to being a Christian, as I see it, with all the rewards that entails, is that one believe in the teachings of Christ, which can be summed up by the three commands to love I mentioned earlier. If that's so, it can little matter what corporate church you prefer to do your worshipping in. I write this as a Protestant Christian but I have no doubt that many of other faiths will see themselves in the picture I have just painted. And when I talk about the teachings of Christ, which I accept for myself, I by no means imply that the teachings of others aren't just as valid as statements of God's will.

Perhaps Queen Elizabeth I put it best, and at a time when ecclesiastical nitpicking was a deadly practice often ending at the stake or the scaffold. She said, "There is only one Jesus Christ—the rest is a dispute over trifles."

Given all that, the church founded by Henry VIII is the one I was born to and I see no reason why it should not be the one I die in. It's as good a clubhouse for followers of Jesus Christ to meet in as any.

MAY I SAY
SOMETHING HERE?

Evidently we're not permitted to speak about abortion any more. Universities—two of them—have in recent years seen their student councils declare that this is a forbidden subject. Politicians—especially of the left—are sent to Coventry if they so much as whisper the "A" word. How come?

There is a moral issue here, dammit, and it ought to be debated. There is no doubt whatsoever that a human life is taken by abortion and it flies in the face of all common sense to argue otherwise. What do the so-called pro-choicers think the woman is carrying, a baby frog? The fetus is alive and it is human. If its albeit tenuous hold on life is to be terminated, surely it must be done in full acceptance of that fact and the consequences.

The debate has been hijacked by the left and others, not on the moral ground but on one of rights. The woman, the asserter, has the right to choice. You see it's easier by far to argue that a fetus has no rights than to argue that it isn't a human life. Therefore the moral argument is shouted down.

But let's be fair. Don't we start with respect for human life as one of, if not the basic tenet of our society? The argument is that the woman carries the fetus and therefore the choice of what she does with her own body is hers alone. But is she just dealing with her own body here? Suppose humans laid eggs—would the female then have the right to kill that unhatched egg?

Silly point it might be said. Women don't lay eggs—but isn't the principle the same? A new life in being has been started and the question is whether that can be interfered with for the convenience of one of its creators.

And that is a point too. It takes two to tango. There is a father in this equation as well. You will probably have guessed by now that I am pro-life. But I am realistic enough to know that women who don't want babies will terminate their pregnancies. I also know that very few if any who do so are free from problems afterwards, like guilt trips and a sense of having taken a life. Psychiatrists' offices are full of women who have difficulty coping with abortion.

The problem with shutting off the debate by saying pro-abortionists are so right that no one else can have a say is that it may well preclude women who experience psychological overtones after abortions obtaining the help many of them will need. If it is just a simple little operation—sort of like having your tonsils out but in another part of the body—why should society care about the aftermath?

The debate has, certainly, become an unpleasant one. Those of deep religious convictions have often made the pregnant woman carrying an unwanted child feel like a social and moral pariah. Logic has gone out the window as the revenge of God is brought into the discussion. The laws of the past have meant that millions of women were killed or badly injured by bungled and amateurish procedures or, all too often, self-inflicted procedures. It is not hard to see how women, fighting for rights against entrenched male ascendancy, would use abortion as one of the battlegrounds.

Surely, though, there is a better way to deal with the issue. Which is, really, unwanted pregnancies.

Back in 1980, when I was health minister for B.C., I went to Minneapolis-St. Paul to look at a program in place in their cities' schools. City and state officials wanted to reduce unwanted pregnancies and knew that bombarding young men and women with moral preachments wouldn't do. They also knew that it was hard for girls to simply walk into a strange adult's office and seek advice. The school district and the health department jointly developed a system of counselling groups that included counsellors for many facets of life—people who could counsel the young on how to buy a car, or seek a certain career path, or solve a personal problem. There was no stigma attached to this group because no one need have any notion about why the young person was going. I tried to get a couple of pilot projects set up in B.C. costing something around $200,000 in all for the province and was turned down by the Treasury Board because I couldn't quantify the results! It was this decision more than any other that sent me down the path to leaving the government. I don't know if this sort of program would have worked—but it sure as hell was worth trying.

Abortion is a huge social problem and it is immensely costly. Not only does the procedure, in the numbers we see them, have a huge impact on the public purse, but we have no way of calculating the cost of the consequences to all involved except to say it must be very high indeed.

I am opposed to abortion on moral grounds. It is simply wrong to take human life at any stage. But I have no wish to see the back-alley abortion return to the scene, and I'm realistic enough to know that this will happen if the procedure is ever again made illegal. We must turn, then, from the impossible to the possible. What can society do?

It can begin to concentrate its efforts better on preventing unwanted pregnancies. This means more effort in schools as well as the home. Better counselling must be made available, and we must start treating this as a problem for all of us, not just the neighbour's daughter.

Of course education is not just for females by any means. It does indeed take two to tango and often the boy is the aggressor and the girl feels obliged to go all the way or lose his love. Hopping hormones work in such a way that sober, temperate second thought is often most unlikely.

But to prevent unwanted pregnancies we must not only dwell on the ways they can be avoided—though that is, of course, critical—but on the consequences that flow from them. And it is here, I think, that the lack of debate has hurt the most. If you listen to the shrillness and godlike certainty of the pro-choice movement, you would indeed get the impression that abortion is little more than a minor operation with no after-effects. That sort of attitude certainly doesn't make the job of the parent or teacher trying to deal with unwanted pregnancies any easier. If you can have unguarded sex with only a minor inconvenience the result of a mistake, what's the big deal?

Talk, as I have, to women who have had abortions—sometimes more than one. There are consequences. Serious ones.

Abortion may have gone away as an argument, but it certainly hasn't gone away as an issue. And it is an issue that society must learn to deal with.

If the Internet Is the Answer, What Was That Question Again?

"What a wonderful world," sang the great Louis Armstrong and I suppose it is. The electronic miracle that has come about since the development of television has changed society so dramatically that anyone who died in the '40s and was reborn today would not recognize the world in which we live. When I think that my mother, who was born the year the Wright brothers made their world-shaking flight at Kitty Hawk, lived to see the nuclear age, a man on the moon, and the computer, I no longer wonder why so many have so much difficulty coping. We've been snowed, folks, and it's going to get much worse. Now don't get me wrong. I have a computer and I'm using it this very second. And it's kind of nice to be able to surf the Internet and get information, make reservations, or just fool around. But it has brought and is bringing consequences that really are uncivil.

It has brought e-mail, "improved" voice-mail, and the 500-, or is it the 1,000- or perhaps 10,000-channel universe.

It has, of course, made communication much simpler and less expensive. And if you think of that just in terms of the cheapness you can call your grandchildren or old friends in faraway places, that seems pretty good. But it has also brought the cellular telephone into every nook and cranny of our lives. At the part of the play, or symphony, when you are most entranced and away from the world around you, phones start to ring. And people actually answer them. You're not free from the phone in church, in the loo, or at dinner. The streets are full of people seemingly talking to themselves until you see that phone stuck in their ear. They're even ringing—and this for me is the last straw—on lakes and streams where the only sound used to be those of nature and whistling fly lines.

Even something apparently as simple as checking in for a flight has been complicated by the computer. Not that long ago I would go out to the airport, go to the checkout line, which was never very long, and, when I got to the front, face this procedure:

"Your name, sir?"

"Rafe Mair."

Following this a quick scan at a list and a tick next to my name.

"Here we are, Mr. Mair. Here's your ticket. We'll be loading at Gate 22 in just under an hour.'

Total time elapsed: two, maybe three minutes max.

Now I go to the airport and there are lines so long that it's impossible to tell which is yours. When you eventually, half an hour later in good times, make it to the front you get:

"Your name, sir?"

"Rafe Mair."

Click, click, click upon dozens of clicks on the computer with, from time to time, serious frowns on the clicker's face, raising for the first time in your mind some serious doubts as to whether or not you're going to fly. Click, click, click upon dozens more clicks whereupon the clerk, without explanation, goes over to talk to a supervisor. Back to some more clicking and miraculously a boarding pass is regurgitated from the computer. Whereupon, after fifteen minutes of the agonies of uncertainty, you are handed your pass and warned that the flight you gave an hour-and-a-half headstart to is loading in five minutes.

The computer can get downright idiotic. A few years ago, I went to the IBM store in Vancouver to get a printing gizmo for my Selectrix typewriter (which dates the story to the days just before the word processor won its war with the typewriter), saw what I wanted in the showcase, and said, "There, that's what I want. I'll take it."

The saleswoman immediately went to her computer. Click,

click, click, etc., etc. and after several minutes sadly informed me they had none in stock.

"But," I protested, "there's one right there in the case!"

"I'm sorry, sir, but our computer shows us that we're out of that particular item. Now if you would like—"

"This is madness," I replied. "There is the typing ball I want—the very one—right there in your case!"

"I'm sorry sir...."

Then there was the marvellous case, when big corporations first started using computers, of the man in England who got a bill from the electricity company for 0 pounds, 0 shillings, and 0 pence. The customer, not unnaturally, decided to ignore this silliness. Each month he got a new bill for 0 pounds, 0 shillings, and 0 pence with increasingly nasty letters enclosing it. Eventually, the utility sent a lawyer's demand note threatening legal action, whereupon our hero wrote the company a cheque for 0 pounds, 0 shillings, and 0 pence. A few days later he received a letter from the company thanking him for his payment.

These bits of idiocy still happen every day, everywhere in the world. This is called the computer age.

In days of yore, there was no voice-mail, no electronic answerers. In those days, to make a call you picked up the phone until "Central," as the always-female operator was called, came on the line within a couple of seconds with "number puleeze," whereupon you gave the number you wished. A few more seconds and the number rang. If you got a busy signal, that was that. No little bell sounded in the ear of the person at the other end telling him or her that someone wanted to break in. And, if there was no answer, that was that too. No one came on and told you whom you had not reached, there was no recording device, and no further options. It was civilized. Laid-back, perhaps, but civilized.

Ah, but, you might say, look how convenient it is now!

I suppose so but I say that, as so often happens, we ruined

a good invention by taking it too far. It ought to be against the law, death penalty for repeat offenders, to have an automatic answerer. Were I king, at the point of entry, in my kingdom, there would have to be a person.

Let me tell you of a recent telephonic adventure I had trying, from my office, without the number at hand, to reach a friend at a national airline in its Vancouver office. After being given the recorded (of course) option press 1 for English or 2 for French, came an endless series of other options. None seemed to fit Public Relations for Western Canada so I tried again. And yet one more time as no category seemed remotely appropriate. I started again. "If you wish service in English, press 1, if you are calling about..." until I heard Media Relations and Corporate Affairs. Now this wasn't exactly PR but it was as close as they'd come so I pressed 1. "This is a recording. Clem Kaddiddlehopper is on vacation until July fifteenth. If you wish his assistant, Ms. Grunge, dial 1." She was either out of the office or on another line so, following instructions I pressed "pound sign," which took me back to option 1, and away I went again!

What to do? I know! I'll go back to the main switchboard and punch in for "reservations." That way I'll get to talk to a "people" and I'll get my friend's number. I did this. Went through the English/French bit again, until I got to "reservations" and pressed 1. Elevator music. And more elevator music. And more elevator music yet. Finally a voice—"All lines are busy. Please hold on until an operator is free. Do not hang up and dial again as staying on the line will be faster." Faster than what? The movement of molasses in winter?

Eventually I got a "people."

"Are you a real person?" was my first and I submit not unreasonable question to the voice at the other end.

"Yes sir, how can I help you?"

"Well, I'm actually trying to reach Ms. X who heads up your PR department—it may be called Media Relations and Corporate Affairs—"

"I'm sorry sir," the lady firmly though politely interrupted. "This is reservations and you'll have to go back to the main switchboard."

"But," I spluttered as I tried to explain how the last forty minutes had played out, "couldn't you just take a moment and give me her number?"

"I'm sorry, sir, that's against company policy." Then more elevator music.

In the meantime, I had put one of my show's producers to work on the matter and she was no further ahead than I.

Lesser folks would have capitulated but we were made of sterner stuff. We put our thinking caps on.

"Ha," I said, "we'll fool the bastards. The British Tourist Authority in Toronto (we were in Vancouver) will have Ms. X's number. Let's call them!"

I explained to the lady on the other end who I was and why it was imperative that I speak to Ms. X soon. I got the number, phoned Ms. X whose phone had been right beside her the whole while, nearly one hour after the exercise had commenced. She said that she detected an edge in my voice! People should phone their own offices some times just for the hell of it— it would be most instructive.

E-mail has ruined the gentle art of correspondence. Yes, it's true that I can now talk with my friends Norm and Chris in Auckland in nanoseconds and for free. There are advantages. But it has also brought clutter. E-mail inboxes full of shit no one cares about and viruses that can knock out your entire hard drive. Worst of all, it has created a sense of urgency.

In my job as a broadcaster I used to receive quite a lot of what we now call "snail mail." I would take an afternoon a week to look it over and answer it. And most of it I answered by hand, though I did cheat a little with a form-letter reply for some. Still, the pace was leisurely. My correspondents didn't expect an immediate response so I could take my time. Now there is not only the sense that you must answer instantly (if you don't, there'll be another e-mail within twenty-four hours asking where the hell your reply is), you must give as full a reply as the length of the e-mail would indicate. It just won't do to say thank you for your e-mail. Your correspondent has taken an hour to dream up a lengthy letter about an editorial or article you've done and you are expected to have the answer back while he's still sitting by his computer! It wasn't easy to send a letter. You had to write it, often by hand, put it in an envelope, find a stamp, and take it down to the post office. Now it's done in an instant and in volume too. I send perhaps ten to fifteen times the mail— hell no, it's much more than that—than I ever did before. And I resent "snail mail" even when it is nice and well thought out. It's too damn much trouble to answer. That's how uncivilized we've become!

And let's talk about this great new entertainment universe. As it is now, my TV watching is confined to the half to three-quarters of an hour per day I'm on the treadmill. I have seventy-four channels to choose from and it's nearly all crap. Sitcoms from twenty years ago, golf infomercials, bad B pictures, professional wrestling, the "best of" a lot of very bad stuff of yesteryear, no end of business advice and weather reports, Oprah reruns. I have virtually no choice but to try to find a news channel for news I've been hearing all day long. Now we're going to get this in the thousands! And it will cost money. There is a mad frenzy in the media world for control of all this. Hugely wealthy companies are spending hundreds of billions of dollars for a bigger share.

Are we any better off than when we had two Canadian channels, perhaps four American networks and PBS? And a VCR for the odd rented movie? Am I happier being assaulted daily by a hundred bits of e-mail at the studio and another twenty on my private address at home—an address that, I might add, doesn't stay private long? Do I need 1,000 alternatives when I'm on my treadmill? Is it all worth the candle?

But worse is to come. All these "services" are going to be

available to you on a hand-held computer. You'll be able to phone out and in, get up on the Internet, e-mail all over the place, look inside your house and see if there's enough cold beer in the fridge. I'm only scratching the surface!

I am not, I assure you, an old fogie. I've been using a computer for nearly twenty years and I admire its efficiency and ability to store what I do in small spaces. And I do have fun on the Internet and I like talking to Norm and Chris more often.

I simply ask about the price, that's all. Shouldn't we declare as quarterly holidays no-computer days? No e-mail. No voice-mail. A closed Internet. Just four days a year? I guess it would not work, though it would be nice to be able to stop this world every once in a while and get off to smell some flowers and cast some line without some damn phone ringing or bell going off to tell me I should consult my pocket computer and check my stocks.

When I was a boy there were a lot of hermits. Some people just checked out and went to live somewhere quiet by themselves. I think the hermit may be making a comeback real soon.

OH! THOSE HABS

I would have made a great hockey player— although perhaps not as great as Mario Lemieux or Wayne Gretsky—but for one bit of bad luck. I never learned to skate. How could I? I was born and raised in Vancouver, which at that time had but one artificial ice rink in the city (ironic considering it also had the first one back in the early years of the century). There was seldom any natural ice, and if there was it lasted only a few days. I did spend a week in Banff when I was fifteen and tried to learn, but all I did was either fall on my ass or splay my ankles so they all but touched the ice. I had to become addicted to hockey through the radio. (All this, I hate to tell you, happened before the telly.)

Every Saturday night I would tune in to CBC radio and listen to the Leafs' games—and hope my little heart out that they'd get their asses kicked.

Why? Because I was an ornery little cuss who didn't like doing as he was told. Which was to be a good little English-Canadian and support the Leafs. You see, in those days, the CBC assumed that only Quebecers wanted to hear the Canadiens games. Even though they were broadcast both on CBC Montreal in English with the incomparable Doug Smith at the mike and in French on Radio-Canada, all anyone outside Quebec could get were Leafs' games. Except one night a year, that is, when the Montreal Canadiens would play their annual Saturday night game in Toronto.

The whole broadcast of Leafs' games, from that bigot of all bigots Foster Hewitt through the "Hot Stove League," reeked with the message that real Canadians—those who spoke

English, sang the "Maple Leaf Forever," and vowed in their version of the national anthem to stay "at Britain's side, whate'er betide"—supported the Toronto Maple Leafs. (Actually the bigger bigot was Conn Smythe who owned the Leafs. He would not permit a French-Canadien to play for them and once began a speech "Gentlemen…and Frenchmen.") Even though no Leaf ever won the scoring title and hasn't to this day (as Casey Stengel used to say, "You could look it up"), patriotic Canadians were supposed to prefer Syl Apps, Ted Kennedy, and Gay Stewart over Toe Blake, Buddy O'Connor, and Elmer Lach who had. Probably the most irritating aspect of these broadcasts came when the Leafs would lose. No matter what the score, according to the "Hot Stove League" the visiting team's goaltender was always the first star, presumably based on the notion that had their opponents not had simply miraculous goaltending the Leafs would certainly have won.

It's strange when you look back from these times. Here was a marvellous rivalry, yet only one side had its games broadcast. Anyone who doesn't think it was straight Ontario-spawned bigotry just wasn't listening.

In the '40s, the bad guys were the colourful Montreal Canadiens. Those were the days of the great "Punch Line" of Maurice Richard and Toe Blake centred by Elmer Lach. They had the great Kenny Reardon partnering Emile "Butch" Bouchard (whose son Pierre would later play for the Habs) on defence and Hall-of-Famer Bill Durnan in goal. And during that decade the Leafs gave them a pretty bad time. (The Habs would get even and then some in the decades that followed.)

It was never easy being a Canadiens fan in those days. Whenever the Leafs beat them for the Cup, as they did in 1947 and 1951, I wanted to hide somewhere. But the next two decades were great. The Canadiens (without the great but injured Jean Béliveau) beat the Leafs in five in 1959, and my greatest day came in 1960 when the Canadiens beat them in the Cup final four games to nothing. The last game was a 4-0 shutout in Maple Leaf Gardens, making it a record five straight Cups for the Habs. (On a sad note, my hero, Maurice (The Rocket) Richard, scored his last goal in that, his final, game.) I walked on a cloud for weeks and sought out my Leaf fan friends (who were for some reason avoiding me) so I could go over the last game minute by minute.

My worst moment came in 1967. I paid a scalper the then-horrendous sum of twenty dollars for a seat for the sixth game won 3-1 by the hated Leafs (with an empty-net goal) giving them the Stanley Cup over my beloved Canadiens. But thereafter it was all roses and the Canadiens dominated the Leafs in the regular season and in the Stanley Cup. In fact, I remember one delicious moment in the '60s where the hated Leaf coach George (Punch) Imlach stated on TV that he hoped the Leafs would meet the Canadiens in the playoffs, implying that the Habs would be sorry if they did. Well, Punch got his wish and the Habs took 'em out in four straight. (I later got to know Punch's son, Brent, a fifth stringer on that Leaf team and he turned out to be a hell of a good guy to my surprise and amazement!)

There is no question that the CBC operated on the theory that it was un-Canadian to broadcast Habs' games outside Quebec, and what this well-entrenched Quebec bashing did was make huge Habs fans out of many in Vancouver. So much so that even in those rare years the Canucks had a decent team, when the Canadiens came to town you'd think they were playing on home ice. I well remember my divided loyalties during one game in the early '80s when my son and I went to a Canucks-Canadiens game. We had standing-room tickets, which were all that was available, and as the game got going I found myself part of a booming chorus of "Go Habs Go!" And me a xenophobic British Columbian!

There is a serious side to all this. The subliminal anti-Quebec message sent out by the CBC and Foster Hewitt tended to create Leaf fans outside Central Canada not because they liked the team but because they felt obliged to hate their arch rivals, the Canadiens, on patriotic grounds. Far from unifying the country, one of the CBC's mandates, it aggravated the cleavage. There was a distinct "anti-Frog" element to cheering for the Leafs.

This almost "racist" rivalry even spilled over into international games when members of the Canadiens and Leafs were playing for Canada. One of my most stressful moments came in the final game of that wonderful 1972 Russia–Canada, eight-game series where the very best of each country met for four games in Canada and four in the former Soviet Union. In the eighth game, the teams were deadlocked at three wins each and one tie. It all hung on the last game, played in Moscow.

For two periods it was awful. Canada, before a world-wide audience, played as if in a trance. Ken Dryden, the Canadiens' all-star goalie was dreadful. The Russkies looked as if they were going to blow Canada out of the rink. Then came the miracle. Dryden was suddenly unbeatable, and with a few minutes to go the great Canadien sniper, Yvan (The Roadrunner) Cournoyer tied it up at five. I doubt there was a Canadian watching that wouldn't have settled for the tie in the game and the series, but it wasn't over yet. A pass from Cournoyer in front and it was suddenly 6-5 Canada and the game was over.

But that bloody goal! It was scored by a Leaf! Paul Henderson of all people. Never mind that the Canadiens' Ken Dryden stoned the Russkies in the last period or that the Canadiens' Yvan Cournoyer scored the tying goal and set up the winner. It was a fucking Leaf who had scored the big one! (Incidentally, Foster Hewitt deliberately mispronounced Cournoyer's name throughout the series.)

Though old habits die hard, I care very little for hockey now. The league is too big, the players never stay put, the salaries are obscene, and the ticket prices too high. But some things never change. If Toronto is in the playoffs, which doesn't happen often, I'm for anyone else. Anyone.

THE LEPRECHAUN

Author's note: On October 16, 1976, my seventeen-year-old daughter Shawn was killed in a one-car motor vehicle accident. I was not aware of the beautiful poetry she wrote until two years ago.

ILLUSIONS?
From up here,
They're all little robots,
Walking, talking, thinking.
All little robots
Blending into society.
They say I am strange, different,
That I have no values.
What are their values?
Food? Clothes? Money?
They say nothing of love or friendship,
They look down on those lower,
And envy those higher.
They're all little robots,
They say I am strange, different,
Not fit for society.
Will they ever know that
It is they who are strange;
All the same,
All little robots,
Forming a society.
I'm not fit for,
Or
Is it a society
Unfit for me?

                                     Shawn Mair, 1976

Seventeen years can be a very long time, I suppose, but when it's a lifetime it can seem so very short. It is, however, long enough to gaze at a brand-new baby and to wonder one more time how this miracle could have occurred out of a pleasure three-quarters of a year before, a pleasure that might have been the result of a fight forgiven, an extra drink or two at the club, a perfunctory bit of sex, or a moment's unplanned passion. It's long enough to see the child grow from utter helplessness to those first efforts at crawling, then the pulling of the chubby body up onto those funny stumpy legs for the first time, the first steps, and the first attempt at running to see Daddy when he comes home at night.

It's long enough to watch a little child develop from a little girl to an awkward pre-teenager when, with her chums, the cacophony of mindless giggles is enough, as my mother would say, to drive a saint crazy.

It's long enough to see a little girl we all called "the leprechaun" start that bond with a father that is such a wonderful part of being a Dad if you're that lucky. And it's long enough to try to sort out all the little jealousies and minor wars that go on with your child and her siblings, a brother and sister one and two years older respectively and a sister two years her junior.

It's long enough to reach that terrible time for fathers when they think they should be playing a role in the teaching that is going on but recognize that for a thousand reasons this is a time when mothers and daughters have to talk and deal with things. It's long enough to see that physical development that just seems to happen and acts like a magnet to young, pimply faced boys reminding you of your own crazy feelings at that age. Embarrassment and puppy love are all too soon followed by the lust that makes fathers hope the youngsters he sees all over his house don't have on their minds what he had on his at their age and that everyone will be knowing and careful.

Seventeen years is long enough to know that here is a person of rare sensitivity who often marches to her own drummer—

but loves the sound of your drums too. It's long enough to see that beautiful young woman in her first formal dress—escorted to the high school graduation dance by that kid with half a beard and a look in his eye that you just don't trust. And it's long enough to be so grateful that everyone got home safely that night.

Seventeen years is long enough to come home one Friday evening, have a couple of drinks, go to bed knowing that all the kids are really too old now to have a full curfew (not that you're relaxed for you never really can be). And it's long enough to wake up with a start at four a.m., for no reason you can later think of, and wonder where she can be at that hour of the night. And it's old enough to get that phone call that all parents live with for a lifetime...there's been an accident...she's dead...and I'm sorry, sir, there is no mistake.

MEMORIES

Will it ever come to pass,
That quick rush of shivers
That runs down my back every time I see you,
That gnawing ache to meet your eyes
As you go by.
My heart pounding furiously every time you speak.
Will it ever come to pass?
I wonder?
Will you ever leave my mind,
And my heart cease jumping,
Every time your name is mentioned.
Will the tears ever stop
Of the memories we spent together?
Oh, how they seem so long ago.
Will you ever leave my mind?
I wonder?

Will I ever forget you?
Your long blonde hair,
And sky blue eyes,
Or were they green?
Your deep masculine voice
Whispering in my ear.
Or was it soft and gentle?
Will I ever forget you?
I wonder,
If I haven't already.

Shawn Mair, 1959–1976

PASSIONS

MY PASSION

I've always said, only half-facetiously, that my knowing nothing about a subject doesn't prevent me from having a strong opinion on it. From the time I can remember, I've always had strong views about things that mattered to me, and I suppose that's one of those good news/bad news sort of things in life. While there is much personal satisfaction from this, you often make it difficult to back off from an opinion you may wish to revisit. I'm not passionate about all things, of course. I haven't too much to say about three-toed sloths, for example. With them it's sort of a live-and-let-live situation. I couldn't care less about cars—as long as they work. When they don't, I can indeed be passionate. There are some things I've been very passionate about that I don't care much about any more—the Montreal Canadiens and the Brooklyn Dodgers which I loved, for example; the Toronto Maple Leafs and Blue Jays, which I hated for another. There are other things I can be passionately indifferent about—television, for one. Most movies, for another. I won't watch the "Oscars" because I'm passionately indifferent to both the medium and the winners.

I believe in passion. It can be easily demonstrated, I think, that lack of passion is what's got our country in so much trouble and what contrasts us, badly in my view, from the Americans, British, and French, to name but a few. Canadians will put up with guff from their governments and authority in general that would take other people to the barricades. We grumble a lot, but when we do get passionate it's usually at others who have done the same. I dare say that on the 1997 APEC issue, where students were pepper-sprayed by the RCMP for protesting Indonesia's Mr. Suharto who attended the APEC Conference at the University of British Columbia, half the country if not more got angry, not at the dictators or the RCMP, but at the students who demonstrated for such controversial things as "democracy" and "free speech." They upset the normal flow of the six o'clock news, where babies born with two heads and cute stray dogs usually dominate, and were tiresome.

Our government can get us into shooting wars—Bosnia and Kosovo for example—without even the usual, ritualistic debate in the Commons and we hardly raise an eyebrow.

Let me demonstrate our lack of passion in another area— sports. Tiny New Zealand, with fewer people than British Columbia, throws its entire population behind its sailors, rugby players, and cricketers. Walk the streets of any city there and you'll hear the test cricket matches coming from radios at virtually every door. Or perhaps it's the America's Cup. Now to me, listening to broadcasts of these two sports is about as exciting as watching paint dry, but when a wicket is taken in a cricket test match you can hear the groans or cheers in the streets. When New Zealand, long the number one world power in rugby, lost to France in the 1999 World Cup, it was a matter of national mourning. So sure were they of victory, the Kiwis had planned a huge parade down Queens Street in Auckland when the All-Blacks returned with the cup as they usually did.

Canadians can, of course, get excited. The entire country did in 1972 when we beat the Russians and Paul Henderson scored that winner in the dying seconds. But it hasn't been all that exciting in any Canada Cup game since. We do, from time to time, temporarily rouse ourselves from our national torpor when someone gets a bronze medal at the Olympics. And we do tend to really perk up for a day or so if we win a gold, but for the most part we're pretty laid-back. Comparatively speaking at any rate.

If we had some passion in our national and provincial souls, we'd never for a moment put up with the kind of governments we have. I don't mean just the quality—goodness knows we could use some help in that regard—but in the system of governance itself. From coast to coast, with scarcely a murmur, we've tolerated systems of government that are about as democratic as the famous trial in *Alice in Wonderland*. Parliaments are exercises in make-believe where prime ministers and premiers do as they please for four or five years yet we docilely go to the polls every four years or so, like bovine masses, and pretend we're taking part in a democratic exercise. They held a tea party in Boston Harbor for considerably less aggravation than we put up with without a whimper year after year.

I believe it can be fairly said that the country we love so much is in grave danger because ours is a love for which we won't fight. It would be sort of, well, un-Canadian to do anything serious about our problems. Oh, we'll flock to Montreal on the eve of a referendum, but that's like the twenty-four-hour flu—there, and really there for a bit, but with no lasting effects.

For passion to be truly effective it must be combined with reason. The American Revolution was indeed won by the Age of Reason led by John Locke, but it needed Tom Paine ("These are the times that try men's souls") too. *The Rights of Man* spelled out what was wrong, but Paine's *Common Sense* brought the pikes out.

We have seen sporadic passion in Canada in recent times. There was indeed the demonstration for Canada in Montreal on the eve of the November 1995 separation referendum as I mentioned. And we saw a pretty good spurt of young passion at the APEC conference. But we have not yet seen the sort of passion that must come if we are to establish, you note I did not say maintain, democracy in this country. Our nation has, in a real sense, suffered because we didn't have a revolution or civil war or both—the crucible from which a people's government emerges. Young people are becoming aware of the terrible "top down" system under which we operate, but I much fear that as they grow older they get too wrapped up in careers to sustain the passionate drive needed, by which time whatever passions we have will be devoted to offshore causes like globalization and genetically modified foods.

It's said, of course, that my generation did show some passion. First in the civil rights movement that really began in the '50s and took fire in the '60s, the feminist movement, which roughly paralleled it, and the consumer rights movement, which was a child of the '70s. The trouble is Canadians were only a few foot soldiers at best. These were American wars led by American leaders with American armies. And Americans are used to taking no crap from authority while we're compliant by nature. Our hero is the single Mountie who kept peace in a Yukon gold mining town or guided, by himself, Sitting Bull and 10,000 braves to the United States border.

For this country to survive it will take more than just a lot of people agreeing that reform should happen and one or two noisy political scientists or talk show hosts playing leader. Our entrenched autocracy has dealt with this sort of activism before and seen it off many times in the past. Examples? The agrarian movements such as Social Credit (Alberta brand), the Progressives, and the United Farmers of Alberta. The "give a dog a bone" method combined with a soupçon of coercion always does the trick, and Ottawa and the provincial capitals go back to business as usual. The fire in the Canadian belly is, sadly, easily quenched.

To have passion one must have, deep in the soul, a commitment to something. In Canada's case it must be that deep commitment to a more just and equitable democracy, where people still have a say the morning after the election and where the disparate regions have power, which is much more than mere representation, at the centre. This passion probably exists in Canadians, but it's buried under a huge pile of reserve layered with modesty and politeness, and spiced by a deeply ingrained respect for authority no matter how abusive. The critical question is whether Canadians can cast off those layers and set aside their inherited preference for drift over action in time to save the country from dying of boredom and lack of will to make things good enough to build a real country on.

FISH ARE WORTH MORE THAN MONEY

I am a conservationist and have the scars to prove it. In June of 1993 I took my radio show (CKNW Vancouver) to Terrace for the day, where I interviewed Bill Rich, then a vice-president of Alcan, a huge, worldwide aluminum corporation that back in the '50s had developed an enormous aluminum refinery and power grid in the northwest of B.C. at Kitimat and Kemano. The subject was the proposed Kemano Completion Plan, which would have reduced the Nechako River to less than 20 percent of its original flow. (The Nechako runs into the Fraser at Prince George and is a vital conduit for the Stuart system sockeye run.) Alcan claimed the right to do this under a 1948 agreement with the Province of British Columbia fortified with enabling legislation.

The interview was a terrible one—the worst I've ever conducted and that covers a hell of a lot of ground. The story is told in my book *Canada: Is Anyone Listening?* and I'll not repeat it here other than to say that by the fall I had become a vigorous if not vicious opponent of the project and ultimately received Canada's most prestigious media award, the Michener, for my efforts.

My "efforts" were really a focal point for the opposition, which crossed cultural, demographic, political, and regional boundaries. There were Indian nations (Carrier) and unions (the United Fishermen and Allied Workers.) There were environmental groups, fishing clubs, and one political party (the provincial Liberals who were, according to the legend of the left, supposed to be in big businesses' pocket). Tough and vocal as they were, however, all these groups and others, as well as all the ordinary people who opposed this project, had no place to vet their spleen—like a radio show with a province-wide audience of up to 350,000 people a week. That I could and did provide. I might say that for my pains I was given a beautiful steelhead rod, reel, and line by the good burghers of Vanderhoof on the east side of the mountains, while the Terrace City Council on the westside declared their bailiwick a "Rafe Mair free zone"! At this writing I'm still not forgiven. Seriously!

I learned a lot from the experience. Mostly I learned that capitalists have suckered us conservationists into a debate we can never win—salmon vs. money. For no matter what price salmon reach on the market, there is no way we can make more money out of them than we can by screwing up their environment. This is why I shudder when I hear well-meaning commercial fishermen, commercial sports entrepreneurs, and sports fishermen talk about how much their three industries contribute to the economy.

If you read Bruce Hutchison's marvellous book *Fraser*, you get a remarkable view of what I called, during the KCP debate, the "soul" of British Columbia—the Fraser River. But even Hutchison, who should have known better, closed his book with the virtues of damming the Fraser. (Dams were a very hot topic just after the Second World War when we were still marvelling at what industrial might could accomplish to achieve flood control and unbelievable amounts of electricity.) I don't blame Hutchison. Alcan was doing Kemano I at the time and the thrill of hydroelectric development was ushering in the W.A.C. Bennett mood of damming a horse peeing if you could get a watt of energy from it. We are all products of our times, and the great Bruce Hutchison was no exception.

Let's get one thing straight right here. There is no way you can dam a river and retain the salmon runs. The Columbia proved that. The problem is not getting the adults past the dam to spawn, it's getting the fry back down the river to the sea. That's a problem that has never been solved and won't likely ever be.

And let's get another thing out in the open—those who would dam rivers don't give a fiddler's fart for the fish no matter how much or how often they bleat to the contrary. They hire accommodating engineers to provide glitzy reports for massaging by excellent spin doctors. They talk of "mitigation," a terrible weasel word that means we destroy a river and give you back a nice big lake full of small mouth bass or some such nonsense. In the '70s, Seattle Light & Power was about to exercise its agreement with B.C. and, by raising the Ross Dam, flood the Skagit Valley on the B.C. side of the border. BC Hydro, because it didn't want to pay the compensation required to buy SL&P off, told us of the wonderful recreation lake this would provide, a lake just ideal for water skiing and jet boating and surrounded with cabins complete with septic tanks. The mitigation the electrical giants always propose seems so hugely expensive, but they are mere drops in the bucket compared to the profits they will reap.

No, we who would conserve our salmonoids, not only our traditional five species of Pacific salmon but rainbows (including steelhead), cutthroat, and char like the Dolly Varden, must frame our arguments on another plane and it need not be complicated.

There may have been a time when we had to destroy salmon to create power, but those days are behind us. We can achieve power from conservation, self-generation by industry, natural gas power, wind power, and tidal power to name but a few. Of course dams are the easiest and probably the cheapest way to go, but we are now, the saints be praised, in the dam decommissioning mode.

This decommissioning is now all the rage in Washington and Oregon, and while it stands as a monument to the doggedness of environmental groups and their Washington, D.C. lobbyists, it is, ironically, raising difficulties of its own. You simply cannot divert the water around the dam, or simply blow it up, without creating very new and substantial habitat problems by very dramatically changing fifty- to one-hundred-year-old water flows that the dams created. This is a study in itself, but suffice it to say that as the hated Army Corps of Engineers who raised the dams in the first place now decommission them, the environmentalists have new battles to fight. But decommissioning, and the sea change in public opinion on dam erection, is a happy thing taking all things into account.

The conservationists' basic argument is unassailable. Salmon and indeed all creatures on this planet are valuable beyond any dollar assessment, just for themselves. When we destroy a salmon run—as we will with the Nechako sooner or later because Alcan has never been forced to make it right by restoring flows (which they can do with the press of a button)—part of us is gone forever. It is part of our geography and biology of course, but it is part of our soul too. We have robbed future generations of something that was rightfully theirs and we have betrayed our trust from God.

This is not an argument of the lofty philosopher. It is, rather, the philosophical argument presented by ordinary people—by natives who rely on salmon for food, by sportsmen who fish for pleasure and as part of a way of life, and by commercial fishermen who rely upon them for their livelihood. But most of all it is the argument of *all* of us—the ones who don't use the resource as much as those who do. The loss of our salmon, however small, is a blot on the heritage that belongs to all British Columbians. They are part of our home.

We can win the fight to keep our fish and restore them to their former glory if we make the battlefield the high ground we occupy. If we go down to the capitalists' level, we lose. We lose hands down because the enormous value we all place on our wonderful God-given gift of salmon cannot and should not be measured in terms of money.

Fishing's Not a Matter of Life and Death—It's Much More Serious Than That

I have never for one moment wondered why I like sex. With girls only. Nor why I like single malt whiskey, Scotch or Irish. Or politics. Or why I love Wendy. But fishing? It drives me nuts sometimes.

I have fished as long as I can remember, starting as a child after shiners off the wharf at Granthams Landing when I was perhaps four or five years of age. When I was in my early teens, I had a bit of a "fish line" at Woodlands on the North Arm of Burrard Inlet combining nascent capitalism with killing fish. I would catch the shiners and put them in a pail as bait for rockfish, which we called rock cod, or for ling cod. (Actually one of the best shiner fishers I ever saw was my uncle's black Labrador, Darky—you'd never get away with that name now, I'll tell you!—who used to wait patiently on the edge of the dock and when a shiner came near the surface would grab it in her teeth and throw it onto the dock. Sometimes you'd come down to the dock and see Darky with a dozen shiners on the dock. Which really is part of this story because, like me, she loved to catch them and she didn't eat them either.)

But back to the pail of shiners. I would then take them in a rowboat around to a corner of the island my uncle and aunt owned and use them as bait for cod. I'd impale one on a big hook, feed the line with the hook and a big sinker to the bottom, pull it up a foot or so, and wait. And I would catch half a dozen cod of perhaps two to three pounds each and occasionally a much bigger ling cod. Then I would clean them by gutting them and pulling the skin off with my teeth. At this point, the world of commerce intruded. I would sell the fillets to the folks in the surrounding summer cabins, use the cod heads in a crab net, and produce fresh crab for our own consumption or perhaps as a special deal for my customers.

At the same time I loved to fish for salmon, and by the time I was in my teens I was a pretty good strip caster or moocher for salmon off my dad's forty-five-foot powerboat. I later graduated to fly fishing. My first fish on a fly was as a boy of ten in 1942 at Lac Lejeune, a famous fly-fishing lake near Kamloops, and when I moved to Kamloops in 1969 I became, so to speak, hooked and got into tying my own flies. I now fish only with a fly and have been lucky enough to do so in New Zealand, England, Scotland, and Ireland, both north and south. But I keep coming back to the question. Why do I do it?

I know I satisfy some primordial instinct to hunt—but is that a good reason when I don't need the fish for food and seldom kill any anyway? I know that I love tying flies and catching fish on my own ties, especially in faraway places, but are those good enough reasons to torment and sometimes kill God's creatures? I know I love the places where fish live, but how does that justify what I do?

I often go through my rationalizations. Jesus didn't object to his disciples fishing and indeed once told them to cast their nets on the other side of the boat for success, which they had in great measure. But then Simon Peter and his buddies were presumably commercial fishermen—did that make a difference? Would Christ approve of a fly fisherman chasing fish for sport?

Yet, so many men of God fish. And women too. One of the earliest writers on fly fishing was supposedly a nun, Dame Juliana Berners. But that scarcely justifies what I do.

I also know that there is little likelihood of much pain involved. I've seen too many hooked fish with no tension on the line swimming about oblivious of the hook in their jaw to believe that there is real suffering. Yet we all know that the experience is scarcely pleasurable from the way they fight when hooked.

Sometimes I compare the fate of the fish I catch to those taken by commercial fishermen. At least I kill mine quickly when I do take one home. Yet the fish in the commercial fisherman's net and those from the fish farm are simply allowed to suffocate, which must be a terrible death. But then, of course, being a logical man I admit that I can't justify a sin by pointing to a greater one.

But I keep on fishing. I look forward to my annual trip to the streams leading into Lake Taupo in New Zealand with even more anticipation than I looked forward to Christmas sixty years ago. I tie flies for this adventure for months before and create my own patterns. My pal Kathy Ruddick, one of the best fly fishermen in the world (she came tenth out of more than a hundred in a recent world championship in Australia, the other ninety-nine all men, incidentally) tells me that I'm a very creative fly tier and, modestly, I am. I'm no hell on the tying part, but I do get a lot of fish on patterns I've adapted myself. Yet for all that, every once in a while when I've landed and perhaps released a good fish, I ask myself the conscience-tormenting question—why did I do that to that poor fish?

I read about fly fishing and have a very considerable library of fishing books by many of the greats all the way from Walton through John Waller Hills to Haig-Brown, and they have all given me the greatest pleasure. Modern writers too like the irrepressible John Gierach—great stuff. I even wrote one myself called The Last Cast. Magnificent entertainment. In fact a very large and legitimate literature has grown up about all types of fishing especially with the fly—and writers better known for other stuff like DeMaupassant, Hemingway, and Zane Grey have left behind classics on fishing. Still, I'm beset with these doubts.

Occasionally I read of a famous or perhaps just well-known fisherman tossing his rods and equipment in the cellar vowing never to fish again. This doesn't, like golf, follow a bad day but comes as an accumulation of deep thoughts that suddenly, like death, reach an irreversible conclusion.

I don't know if that will happen to me. As I get older, my conscience seems to bother me a bit and I find myself more and more taking refuge in all the rationalizations I've mentioned and some I haven't. Yet some of the finest people I've ever met—both people who are great characters and have great character—have fished happily to the end of long lives. I think of the late Barney Rushton and the late Jack Shaw in Kamloops; Ralph Shaw (no relation, formerly of Kamloops and now on Vancouver Island); and, of course, the great Roderick Haig-Brown of Campbell River. And the many still living like Steve Raymond, Dave Hughes, and my friend Keith Draper in New Zealand. And I'm comforted just as a drunk is comforted in the knowledge that there are plenty of other barflies in the world.

But I still ask myself questions I can't answer. And I'll probably go on fishing secure in the knowledge that if the fish are going to get even with me in another lifetime, or in the hereafter, there are enough of them now to keep me tormented for several millennia and plenty more that outwitted me and would much enjoy watching my discomfort. But then you never know. I might—at a time when I least thought it would happen—look down at a beautiful four-pound rainbow lying at my feet and say, to hell with it, I think it's the garden for me.

But if you're a betting person, don't bet on it!

A FLY ON THE WATER

I love to fish with a fly. In fact, I've invested a considerable amount of time, energy, and money—especially the last—on this the pastime of my advancing years.

I'm not sure why I like to fish, but I know that when I was a very small boy I was enchanted by the shiners that darted around under the wharves—floats more properly—at Granthams Landing where my family spent its summers in the '30s. I was a very little boy then, but I've been blessed with a pretty good memory of my childhood, which speaks of happy times even though it was a Depression time. I well remember the Union Steamship rides to Granthams from Vancouver on the *Lady Cynthia*, the *Lady Cecilia*, and the *Capilano*, and I have a very vivid memory of a trip home when I was allowed to "steer" and then bunk down in the captain's cabin.

I remember the first two "sea trout"—as small salmon were then called—I caught with my parents off Gower Point. They fished with big cane rods and large spoons, and I had a hand line with a small Gibbs and Stewart "Tom Mack" or "Diamond," spoon designed for the smaller fish, on the end of the line. We stopped for lunch just behind what was known as "Salmon Rock" on Keats Island that day. I know that because I recognize the place from a picture my mom took of me proudly holding my two fish, and from a later visit as a teenager with my girl-friend, a visit noted for much more than a sandwich lunch. I also well remember the time a salmon (probably a coho) hit my hand line and burned my fingers as the line zinged through them.

It's funny what you remember. My dad had an old Evinrude

outboard that was started by a rotating handle on the top of the shaft. (Engine people will forgive my lack of technical knowledge, but while my teenage friends learned about engines, I pursued the delights that led to luncheons and other things in the little bay behind Salmon Rock on Keats Island with my girl.) In any event, my father used to grab this little handle and spin the top of the engine until it started—which it often did not, giving me an early appreciation of the fullness and depth of the English language in the vernacular. And though there was only one handle, two appeared when the top of the engine was spinning and I could never then, and can't now, understand why.

When I was about thirteen my dad gave me a small outboard for my dinghy—also an Evinrude but with an automatic starter cord. He presented me with a crescent wrench as well. I asked him what this was for and he said, "Two things, my son. To change the spark plug with when necessary, and to hit the fucking thing with when it won't start." Over the months ahead I was surprised how often a reluctant motor would respond to a smart smack on the side with that wrench.

Childhood fishing became a lifelong love, which, in my late thirties became a passion for fly fishing including tying flies.

Fly fishing is not as complicated as it looks—it's far worse than that. What starts out as thrashing the water with what better anglers tell you is the "right pattern" becomes a love not just of the fishing and the fish but the ecology. All fly fishermen of any note become amateur, and indeed sometimes-professional, entomologists. The passion takes you under water into a study of what lives there and what they look like. Dragonfly and damselfly nymphs are scrutinized with great care. So are mayflies and caddis. In the late '60s, fishing the tiny midge, or chironomid, became all the rage, which it remains to this day. Added to that are freshwater shrimp and leeches. Then there are terrestrials like grasshoppers, bees, and, in New Zealand, the ubiquitous cicada.

All fishing is mostly about observing things. There is a reason why some people always outfish others—they see things, take note, and make adjustments. Whether you're a kid fishing for shiners or an Ernest Hemingway type fishing for giant tuna, you'll succeed where others don't if you keep your eyes open and your wits about you.

What I've always found so frustrating about my fishing is that I can sometimes be so very good at observing things that I indeed often outfish others around me. Then I can wake up one day after years of fishing a certain place a certain way and find that I've missed what is so obvious. And that's probably what makes fishing such a challenge and so frustrating. You can look back at days you thought were wonderful but, because you finally opened your eyes, those same days now fill you with a sense of loss. When I look back upon times of greatest joy—and deepest frustration—as a fly fisherman, those memories take me to one of the true fly-fishing meccas of the world, New Zealand.

My father was a New Zealander (which happily gives me dual citizenship), and my direct love affair with that place began in 1981. My first fishing experience there, with a very fine and well-known fisherman and writer called Keith Draper, was brief, but the following year I returned. Before doing so, I corresponded with the Taupo Flyfishers' Club and its president Keith Wood because I wanted to tie my own patterns. It turned out Keith owned a motel at Four Mile Bay on Lake Taupo, the country's biggest lake, and was a fishing guide as well. Thus started a ten-year friendship that only faded when Keith sold his motel, moved around the lake to Kinloch, and took up selling real estate. Keith was a hell of a good fisher-man and guide, which shows that for all the glamour it's seen to involve, guiding is not much of a money-maker.

At that time, upstream nymphing had become all the rage and had largely replaced the downstream wet fly fishing that had been the fashion on rivers near Taupo. Keith initiated me into what some, with a sneer, call fly fishing with a float.

The technique is to cast the weighted nymph pattern, usually imitating a caddis worm, upstream and let it drift without any drag, that is to say, free of influence from the current on the line that would cause an unnatural drift. With the help of a bit of coloured wool where the line is attached to the leader, you can see when a fish touches your nymph. When the wool so much as twitches, you strike.

It's tough fishing, nymphing. Generally you cast two nymphs, the trailer, a small fly representing a mosquito-like nymph called a chironomid, attached to the bend of the hook of the second, larger fly. The cast is difficult because it must be done so there is no "whipsaw" effect. You want the line to mimic the natural drift of the nymphs while at the same time, if you allow the line to become too slack, you will not be able to strike promptly when the strike indicator dips. It's truly an art not to be disparaged and, when you're fishing only ten days or so a year, is difficult to master. I've become pretty good at it, but for the first couple of days each year I'm a basket case, hanging up continually on trees across the stream and behind me. Or getting those two damned flies gloriously mated so that the end of the line is a mass of tangled nylon and the two flies are trussed up with a finality only scissors can part.

My trips to New Zealand became annual events and I got to know, reasonably well, all four of the principal rivers draining into Lake Taupo: the Waitenahui, the Hinemaimai, the Tauranga-Taupo, and the Tongariro. And as the years passed, my wife Wendy and I settled on the Tauranga-Taupo as our favourite.

The T-T, as it's colloquially called, is the loveliest stream in the world and I'll brook no argument on that subject. It's a gravel river, heavily punctuated with pumice stone. In other words you don't have to negotiate huge boulders, which is your lot if you fish the more famous and nearby Tongariro. The banks are full of toe-toe, the local version of pampas grass, which has the anthropomorphic habit of stretching out and grabbing any fly that comes within a few metres of it. As you progress upstream, the banks become steep cliffs making one feel as if in a large Gothic cathedral. In fact, I started calling one such pool the Cathedral Pool and the name has stuck with the locals.

I have had some wonderful fishing along this most wonderful of streams but until recently had done very little "dry" fly fishing, which is to say with a floating fly imitating either a hatching insect or a terrestrial. In fact, it was not until my seventeenth year down there that guide Graham Dean suggested we try fishing dry with a cicada pattern, which we did one day on the lower Tongariro with mixed success.

The cicada is a big cricket—about half again as big as a bumble-bee—and spends most of its life underground. They hatch in hot weather and make a hell of a racket all day and all night. If one wasn't able to tune them out they would drive you bonkers.

As with humans, sometimes for cicadas shit happens and they are blown out of the nearby willow trees into the water where they become a delicious and calorie-filled meal for hungry rainbows and browns. And here, finally, I've reached the point of my story. How come I hadn't noticed this before?

I had become, as humans do, such a creature of habit and prejudices that I would thrash the water with nymphs on baking hot days, with the cacophony of a million cicadas ringing in my ears, and never notice the occasional "slurp" indicating that another delicious and most vulnerable meal had been eagerly absorbed by my stubborn prey. Because these large insects didn't hatch in the water as mayflies and caddis do, I had never noticed them. It was as if I were a birdwatcher in spring and had failed to notice the robins.

But it's not just me. You can scour the many books written about fishing in New Zealand—and there is a delightful literature on the subject—and find nary a word about fishing cicadas. Even the estimable Norman Marsh, the best of the Kiwi writers on matters entomological, only mentions the cicada casually, concentrating much more on hatching mayflies.

So the next year Wendy and I made a vow. We would perform

that most difficult of disciplines—we would fish dry, with a cicada pattern, no matter if we spent all day fishless. That's a tough vow to keep, especially if you have spotted fish and you can't raise them.

Fishing New Zealand rivers in the summer is tough sledding at the best of times. There simply aren't a lot of fish in the rivers—they really start to move up around June, the beginning of winter. But there are fish. And my theory is that the steelhead from Sonoma Creek, planted in Taupo nearly a hundred years ago, have developed a strain we would call summer steelhead. There is spawning in January and February as any who have hiked upstream can attest.

Normally, I would be delighted to take three fish on a hot January day and there have been many days I have been skunked or been content with a couple of fish hooked and lost. Our first day pledged to fish cicadas only took us to a lovely stretch of water not far from the point where you must abandon the car. I went downstream from where the trail ended and Wendy took the first pool upstream. Before I had even reached the point I wished to start I looked upstream and Wendy was into a fish. Damn! I thought, I'll bet that woman has cheated and put on a nymph!

I went down to the bottom of the run and cheated a bit myself. Hell, she must be cheating, so why not? Besides, I did not really cheat. I just attached a little pheasant-tail nymph to the cicada pattern—to sort of have it both ways—and cast upstream into the middle of the stream, about ten or twelve metres out. After about half a dozen casts, boom! Into a very nice rainbow who dashed up and down the pool. I could see he'd taken the cicada, and that was soon confirmed as the trailing nymph hung up on a sunken tree. My just deserts!

I waded out to the tree, with the water lapping over my chest waders, loosened the pheasant-tail nymph, and was surprised indeed to find the fish still connected to the dry. I beached and released a lovely three-pound hen, then proceeded to hook five more, all on the cicada (I'd stopped cheating!) all before lunch. When we met for our lunch break, it turned out Wendy had been just as lucky.

We fished for eleven days all told, eight of them in this lovely mile and a half stretch and had the same marvellous fishing every day.

All of a sudden my eyes, like a two-week-old kitten's, opened up. Where I had seen nothing in past years, now I saw these big buggers dropping all over the stream and being gobbled up by waiting trout. The strike is not a particularly hard one. The fish seem to know there's lots of time because the cicada has no chance of becoming airborne again. They are clumsy flyers and very splashy swimmers, meaning the trout can simply swim up lazily from the bottom and, with a quick clomp, have a hearty meal. Occasionally you do hear a noisy take, and I suspect that's when two trout are eyeing the same morsel. But there I was, an eighteen-year veteran on the Taupo rivers, fishing the way I like to fish best for the first time.

Now, this wasn't the first year cicadas fell on the water making full meals for lazy trout, and it got me thinking. Perhaps an axiom for fly fishermen to follow is this—the people who write about fishing either don't pay very careful attention to detail or they know something they don't care to have you know.

To this a postscript—the locals don't always tell you everything either. A year later Wendy and I made our usual trip and for the first four days it poured rain, making the rivers unfishably high. We tried a couple of the river mouths without much success and really felt more than just a bit glum. Now you must remember that we've been fishing these parts for nearly twenty years so when Peter, our host where we stay, casually mentioned the Kuratau River mouth I asked, with no little surprise, where the hell that was?

"Oh," replied Pete, "it's about half an hour from here. Paved road. Can't miss it, give it a try."

With nothing to lose, Wendy and I did just that. And we

found the most fabulous river mouth and knocked 'em stiff for the three days it took for the rivers to go back down to being fishable.

"What the hell, Pete," I exclaimed when I got back—I may be forgetting a couple of expletives here—"why in God's name didn't you tell me about this earlier? Like in 1985?!" He just smiled and shrugged. After all, the locals had to save something for themselves. It was just the same old story—if we're not careful, in fishing as in life, we assume that the knowledge we have is all the knowledge available on the subject.

JACKIE ROBINSON LIVES!

I have, for as long as I can remember, been a baseball fan. I can't explain it but it is so. Some of my clearest childhood recollections are of sitting by the radio listening to the World Series, the first one being between the Dodgers and Yankees in 1941 when Mickey Owens dropped the third strike and let the Yankees turn a sure loss into a win.

It's so long ago now. And our need to remember seems dulled by the great black athletes we see all around us. When you look out especially on the basketball courts and baseball diamonds of today it's hard to remember that blacks were not terribly welcome in the former and not welcome at all in the latter until 1947.

Most of you reading this won't have any memory at all of baseball pre-1947 when, in the major leagues, it was whites only. Those were the days of the great Ty Cobb, Babe Ruth, Tris Speaker, Rogers Hornsby, Walter Johnson, and Bob Feller. In 1947 itself, baseball featured the likes of Joe DiMaggio, and Ted Williams. And there were other greats like Stan Musial, Pee Wee Reese, and Whitey Ford. The last name perhaps summed it all up—they were great players, but they were all white.

We knew about the Negro Leagues all right. We had heard about Josh Gibson and Satchel Paige, and some of us had seen the latter play exhibition games with the touring House of David. We'd heard that Paige had struck out the great Babe Ruth three times in an exhibition game. But they weren't really the major leagues, now, were they? How could they be?

I remember 1947 very well. I was sixteen and the war had ended two years before. Like most kids my age, I had listened to the propaganda of the war and had taken it seriously. The war was fought for the brotherhood of man. We would see the end of discrimination. There would be equality. Gone were words like "chink," "nigger," and "kike." It was a perfect era for teenage idealists—which we all were.

It was the perfect time too for a tight-fisted general manager named Branch Rickey of the Brooklyn Dodgers, He was the man who decided that this white-only stuff had to stop and in 1946 signed a twenty-five-year-old black player from the Kansas City Monarchs (of the Negro League) named Jackie Robinson and sent him off to play with the Dodgers' farm team, the Montreal Royals of the Triple A International League.

Jackie Robinson had been a three-sport threat at UCLA: an All American football player, a track star (it ran in the family for his brother had been on the 1936 American Olympic team and ran second to the great Jesse Owens in the 100-metre dash), and a baseball star. Many knowledgeable people say Robinson was the greatest American all-round athlete of them all—even better than Jim Thorpe.

Jackie Robinson did everything expected and more with the Royals, leading the league in hitting. Now, having started the experiment, Rickey had to finish it and the next year Robinson was brought to the big team.

It is interesting to note why blacks had been excluded. There were social reasons, of course. No southern white boy would play with a "nigra" on the team. Where they came from everyone "knew their place," especially "nigras." And how could you possibly expect teams in the south to accept "niggers"?

And there was another reason. Why negroes, it was well known, were cowards. They had a yellow streak down their back. The first time a Bob Feller threw a pitch at his head (in this pre-helmet era) why the negro would run for cover and never step into the batter's box again. So it was solemnly intoned. That, the southern whites told all who would listen, was the real reason that "nigras" didn't belong in the majors.

Rickey knew different. He had seen the wonderful players in the Negro Leagues and in fact knew of better ballplayers there than Robinson. There was Sam Jethroe for one. There was Monte Irvine, Roy Campanella, Luke Easter, Hank Thompson, and, of course, the legendary Satchel Paige. But Rickey knew that Jackie Robinson was the best man to be the first man. He not only had the talent but the maturity of a man who had been one of the first blacks to be an officer in the U.S. Army. He knew that Robinson, a passionate man, nevertheless could display the patience it would take to be the first black in the Majors where he'd been court-martialed for defying the colour ban. And so it proved to be.

The St. Louis Cardinals threatened to strike rather than play against Robinson but Baseball Commissioner A.B. "Happy" Chandler, himself a southerner, threatened to suspend the lot of them and they played. Enos Slaughter, a mean spirited southerner but a hell of a ball player, got his revenge by sliding into first base and spiking Robinson. (Robinson, who played second base next to Pee Wee Reese, the Dodgers' Hall of Fame shortstop, for most of his career played first base in his rookie season.) Slaughter never made the Hall of Fame and this is thought by most baseball experts to be the reason.

The Dodgers' star centre fielder, "Dixie" Walker, allowed as though he'd rather not play with a black and Rickey promptly traded him to Pittsburgh.

On Robinson's first day there was a huge crowd at Ebbets Field and one of the better stories has it that as he left his apartment, Robinson kissed his wife Rachel and said "Honey, when you look down on the field, you'll recognize me—I'll be wearing number 42."

Jackie Robinson went on to a sparkling career. He was Rookie of the Year in 1947 and two years later won the batting title with a .342 average and was the league's Most Valuable Player. Among his many talents, he became one of the most feared "clutch" hitters in baseball. And, after Rickey released him from his pledge to turn the other cheek, Jackie Robinson became a man no one messed with. Ever.

Branch Rickey's payoff came in 1955 when his Dodgers, led by a now-aging Jackie Robinson, went from two games down to beat the hated Yankees and win their first World Series. By this time, there were a number of black stars. Roy Campanella, Don Newcombe. Sam Jethroe, Luke Easter, Hank Thompson, and Monte Irvine had all made it. So, finally, had Satchel Paige. So had a kid named Willy Mays.

There was an incident in 1951 that said it all about Jackie Robinson, the competitor. The Giants, thirteen and a half games behind the Dodgers, had made up all that ground and at the end of the season, the teams were tied. With the three game playoff tied at one each, and the Dodgers leading the third game 4-2 in the bottom of the ninth, Ralph Branca served up a gopher ball to Bobby Thompson who hit a three-run homer to beat the Dodgers 5-4 and thus win the pennant. The place was bedlam, but as the rest of the Dodgers slunk off the field, Robinson followed Thompson around the bases making sure he actually touched every base. The man did not like to lose.

It's all very different now. We've seen the likes of Bob Gibson, Roy Campanella, and Ernie Banks. We've watched in utter amazement as Ozzie Smith made plays no one else ever made. We saw Hank Aaron become the all-time home run king and in 1998 we watched as Sammy Sosa beat Roger Maris's single-season homers mark but got beaten for the title by a guy named McGwire who hit seventy of them.

For all under a certain age it's utterly impossible to imagine baseball without black players. How could such talent have been excluded for so long?

Well, it was and all baseball's records prior to 1947 ought to have an asterisk indicating that they were made before blacks were allowed to say something about them.

Before 1947, there was no telling how good major leaguers were because some of the best ball players in the world were not permitted to compete. Jackie Robinson changed all that. Not only does every black player since owe an irredeemable debt to Jack Roosevelt Robinson, so does all of professional sports.

Why I Love London So!

L ondon is a magical city. I visit it three times a year. Regular. Like clockwork. When asked some years ago by a colleague why I was going to London yet again I replied, why not? Is there a better place to be for a vacation?

Many Canadians visit Hawaii, or Mexico or the Caribbean regularly. They often have condos there—or perhaps in Palm Desert, California, or Hilton Head, South Carolina. They would be amazed to be questioned about why they go to these places as often as they can. Yet I can't understand why they're not off to London. Different strokes for different folks, I guess.

My love affair started as a child with A.A. Milne's Christopher Robin and friends (I always saw myself as Eeyore —still do). I saw Buckingham Palace in my mind's eye when "Christopher Robin went down with Alice." As a child I was taught by a marvellous old English soldier, Captain Robinson, at St. George's School in Vancouver. I saw, through him, the prison hulks in the Thames as described by Dickens and Kensington Gardens of Peter Pan fame. During the war I saw, in my mind's eye, the flames leaping around St. Paul's Cathedral and the House of Commons wrecked by the Luftwaffe.

My army of toy lead soldiers so cruelly cut off by the Second World War curtailment of their manufacture was another link to this city of my dreams. I was enchanted, in absentia, by Poet's Corner in Westminster Abbey, by Samuel Pepys watching the Great Fire from the tower of All Hallows, by Traitor's Gate where the then-Princess Elizabeth (later Elizabeth I) was taken to the Tower of London and, of course, by the Bloody Tower itself.

I had in my mind's eye images of the docks of London in flames during the Blitz in 1941, of Pudding Lane where the Great Fire of 1667 started, and, as I moved through life into law school, the great legal battles in the Old Bailey and the Royal Courts of Justice. I am, unashamedly an Anglophile and, if there is such a word, a Londonphile.

My first trip to London did not come until February 1964. I'll never forget flying over the English Channel and wondering where all the people were as I looked at this green carpet below me. Then I saw London and it was like a dream on this beautiful cold February morning as we came right above all the great sights of London. There was the Tower, St. Paul's, and the Parliament Buildings all so clear.

I checked into the hotel, and quickly asked where Buckingham Palace was. "Right down Park Lane, sir, and down Constitutional Hill—you can't miss it." What he didn't tell me is that it was about two miles away. My walking shoes were a pair of Oxfords, not the best of walking shoes, and it was that day I learned that, for what reason I cannot tell, London has the hardest pavement in the world!

I walked and walked as if I were in a trance. I wasn't at all tired despite having been up for a day. I was too damned excited to be tired. I got to Buckingham Palace just as the Guards (in grey because it was winter) were changing. I couldn't believe my luck. Then I walked through St. James's Park to Westminster Abbey, which I could only just look at quickly. Then out into Parliament Square and the Parliament Buildings with Big Ben. I walked up Parliament Street, through Whitehall to Trafalgar Square, and there he was, just as I had imagined, my boyhood hero Nelson on top of his huge column. I went through Trafalgar Square and just had to find Piccadilly Circus, which I did, stopping at B.C. House at No. 1 Regent Street (a place I would in later years spend a lot of time at) to sign the guestbook. I then walked up Regent Street to Oxford Circus, and down Oxford Street to Marble Arch and my hotel. And this part I will never

ever forget. I simply could no longer walk a foot. My legs were ramrods at the knees and my feet were raw. And I had not eaten. I got to my room and called room service for a sandwich and some Epsom Salts, then drew a bath, soaked in the Epsom Salts, and ate my first nourishment. I felt like I had died and gone to heaven.

I recovered sufficiently to find my way to my first British pub—the Old Quebec round the corner from the hotel, where, for the first and only time in my life, I was propositioned by a man.

I didn't return to London until 1972 and was there again in 1974 and 1975. But from 1976 on, I have averaged at least three trips a year—I reckon about seventy to eighty trips in all. And I still haven't had enough of the place.

London is like an artichoke—you just keep on peeling off the layers. But you must be patient. To do a guided tour of Westminster Abbey takes about an hour. To see it properly takes at least half a day. Thoroughly, several days. St. Paul's, including the crypt and a visit to the inside of the dome called the Whispering Gallery, which is not for people like me with acrophobia, takes a couple of hours. The Tower of London with a Beefeater guide and the Jewel House with the Royal jewels takes a good two to three hours. And when you've done that—and one per day is all you want to do—you have not even begun to scratch the surface of London. Not by a long shot.

There are the obvious things, of course. Any London guide book will tell you about them: Buckingham Place, Big Ben, and the lot. Some you can easily pass without missing a thing—Madame Tusseaud's, for example. Other less publicized ones like the Public Records Office in Chancery Lane, which contains the Domesday Book amongst other documentary treasures, and the Cabinet War Rooms where Churchill spent so much time during the Blitz are musts. The "must" list is never-ending.

There are museums for all tastes. The City of London Museum in the Barbican is a wonderful walk through the city's history and it is actually bounded, in part, by the old Roman wall that once completely encircled the city. There is the wonderful Wallace collection of paintings, sculptures, and, above all, ceramics and china. If you're a fan of the French Impressionists then you must go to the Courtauld Gallery at Somerset House on the Strand.

There is the theatre—the highlight of which is the new Globe Theatre in Southwark, constructed just as the old Globe owned by Shakespeare was, and only a couple of hundred of yards from the original site. Any time from May through September you can see Shakespeare as it should be seen—some of the audience in the stalls but a large portion in the open air "pit" where they exchange insults with the players.

Some things in London take forever to find out about. For example, a piece of wonderfully preserved pre-fire, indeed Elizabethan architecture at St. Bartholomew-the-Great Church near the old Smithfield Market is a gem you'll never read about in the tour manuals or see on any guided tour. Its preservation is a story in itself.

After the Great Fire in 1667, Charles II ordered that all the casements, the overhanging windows, be plastered in. The reasoning was that these overhanging casements had caused a wind tunnel that had allowed the fire to quickly spread. In the First World War, Germany bombed London from zeppelins and a bomb dropped on the street just outside the courtyard of St. Bartholomew-the-Great Church (which some argue is London's oldest) and dislodged all the plaster on the building that houses the passageway leading from the street to the church. Behind the plaster was the most perfectly preserved Elizabethan architecture you could possibly imagine. Many tourists pass through the archway to the wonderful old church yet never notice this casement!

Over the years I have undertaken personal missions. One year I decided to look at all the Wren churches in London. I didn't make it for they are far too numerous but I made a fascinating discovery. Sir Christopher Wren wasn't an architect at all, he was an astronomer, but he was called upon to rebuild London after the fire and his pièce de résistance, of course, was St. Paul's. What is not known, I daresay, by one in a thousand tourists who visit this magnificent cathedral, is that a few yards away, down Ludgate Hill, is the tiny church of St. Martin's Ludgate. It is constructed so that you can't see the church proper from the street even though its entrance is right on Ludgate. It was built by Wren to show the insignificance of man while St. Paul's was built to the greater glory of God. It has a number of interesting features, one of which is the false wall built to keep out the noise from the street and when you think of it, in the late 1600s and early 1700s, the streets were all cobblestone and the carriage wheels all iron—it must have been a hell of a clatter!

Another year I retraced the steps of the great diarist of the Restoration period, Samuel Pepys, who is also, rightly, considered the Father of the Royal Navy. His church, St. Olaves, is still there amidst the concrete and steel edifices that surround it. And so is Seething Lane where he lived and worked. The church steeple from which he watched the Great Fire, All Hallows-by-the-Tower, is still there too, although it, like so many other churches, was carefully reconstructed, brick by brick, after the Blitz. My wife Wendy and I attended Sunday Matins at both churches on one of our trips.

Covent Garden is a wonderful place to visit on a Sunday where, in the café in the basement, you will hear marvellous singers and stringed quartets. A bob or two for the pot and this is, without any doubt, the best entertainment value in London.

London is above all else a walking city and it has the most wonderful walks. You can even take guided walks—several of them in fact—though I've never taken one. I prefer to plot my own course, which probably doesn't surprise you. I start one of our favourite private walks by taking the Underground to Notting Hill Gate, then walking through Kensington Gardens, past the Peter Pan statue, of course, into Hyde Park and along the Serpentine, crossing at Hyde Park Corner to Green Park, then over the Mall through St. James's Park to Parliament Square and Westminster Abbey. A long walk indeed—but in what other city could you have a walk like that right in the middle of town?

Another favourite is taking the tube to Hampstead Heath where the walks are exquisite and hold, on a clear day, unbelievable views of the City below. Hampstead itself is a small village within Greater London and is fun in its own right. Next door another village, Golders Green, is named after the goldsmiths of medieval times and to this day is very Jewish. If you've a mind, you can go to Karl Marx's grave nearby.

Yet another of my favourite walks starts at Big Ben and takes you across Westminster Bridge and east along the Thames until you reach Tower Bridge. This is called the Albert Embankment and gives, in addition to the flavour of the Thames, wonderful views of the City of London. Another favourite starts at Sloane Square along King's Road to Chelsea, then through Cheyne Walk along the Chelsea Embankment up through the Sir Christopher Wren-designed Royal Hospital for pensioners of the armed services, and back to King's Road.

There is, of course, the shopping—Harrods, the world's most famous (rightly) department store in Knightsbridge, Selfridges on Oxford, and so many others up Regent Street and down Oxford. For the fisherman there are the traditional Hardy's and Farlow's (both now owned by Hardy's) on Pall Mall, though I'm bound to say that the superior marketing skills of Americans at Sportsfish on Pall Mall smack in between them as well as Orvis on Dover Street are showing them all up.

I have scarcely touched upon the wonders of London, but I hope I have made you understand why, when my friends hop over the water to Maui or go down to Palm Desert, I'm off, rain or shine, winter, spring, summer or fall to London—the greatest city in the world.

I Am a Bookaholic

They say you can tell a lot about a person by his library. I have to wonder what people would say about me had they only my library of about 2,000 books to help them judge me. I have very few classics—I did have the Franklin Library's one hundred greatest books and all the Pulitzer Prize winners until the early '70s, but they went missing in a divorce. I have endless biographies, most fairly modern: two of Wellington, three of Nelson, and ninety-five about Winston Churchill, who has a special section. There are three on Hitler, three on Napoleon, and two on Thomas Paine. There is a section devoted to Canadiana of course, and a special section for political comment by the likes of George Will and general comment by the wonderfully articulate Bernard Levin. The largest section, apart from biographies, and just nudging the three hundred mark, is on fly fishing, which has most of what Roderick Haig-Brown ever wrote, a first edition of Negley Farson's classic *Going Fishing*, and a dozen of the Fly-fishing Classics series, which cost a fortune but which are so beautiful. I'm mildly proud to say I have two books of my own in this collection: *The Last Cast*, a fishing book, and *Canada: Is Anyone Listening?*, a book about Canadian politics. As I look up from my computer, I can see a shelf of eight books that, when added to the seventeen piled on chairs, constitutes the current unread pile.

Have I actually read all these books? Mostly, though I'm embarrassed to see some of them with bookmarks sticking out indicating that I didn't quite make it all the way. I read four books at a time. One is in my office/study, one by my chair in the living room, one by the biffy, and one by the bedside.

Where on earth do I get these books? The major source is London. Wendy and I are there three times a year, and I take an extra duffel bag to bring the books home with me. I'm no sooner there when I'm in Hatchards on Piccadilly or Foyles on Charing Cross Road like a kid in a candy store not quite sure where to begin. Now of course the old Simpsons department store on Piccadilly has been taken over by Waterstone's and is, so they say, the largest bookstore in Europe with five floors of books and restaurants. To be there is like I died and went to heaven.

I used to start out by buying perhaps eight or ten books on my first day, but now I do try to move more slowly and save my strength so to speak. But at the end of the trip I still have at least one duffel bag of books. I'll bet I'm one of the very few who come back to Canada having to pay GST on books.

I don't have much of monetary value. I do have a Canadian first edition of Churchill's *History of the English-Speaking Peoples* and a remarkable limited edition, for which I paid about $1,250, of all his writings other than his books and speeches. It is a wonderful four-volume set that gives you all the articles he wrote during the three decades or so that he was Britain's highest-paid journalist. But the value of my books cannot be measured in monetary terms.

Non-bookaholics cannot understand how one can have scores of books in one's possession that have yet to be read while still buying new books like mad. The answer is uncomplicated— we bookaholics simply love books. We get a simple but deep pleasure just being surrounded by our books. I know that I'll never take most of them off the shelves except when it's time to reshuffle them to restore their alphabetical order, but that does-n't matter. What matters is that they're there. Of course, there's some utility here too—as a journalist there is very little I need to know that can't be found in the books I possess.

From time to time I houseclean, determined to get rid of books that not only don't have any intrinsic or aesthetic value but are simply clutter. I start this process with the vigour of a man on an unpleasant task—I hate it but I know it must be done. Books come flying off their shelves into a pile on the floor to be put in boxes for a future garage sale. Then, of course, comes the final culling just to be absolutely sure, don't you know? These are old friends that I once had a deep, if fleeting, affection for. I once took them off a bookstore shelf, carried them to the counter, and made them mine. So, traditionally, I look at these potential discards, and one by one they go back on the shelves until I'm left with, perhaps, five to be executed. Three of those will be duplicates—I'm damned if I know how I can buy two of the same but I do—and the others? Hell, they're not doing any harm really so I put them back. The extra copies I give to my daughter Cindy who will, no doubt, wonder why I think she wants Lord Jenkins's biography of Asquith or yet another book on Churchill.

There is a serious point to all this idle chatter about books because the nerds of the world tell us that books will soon be passé. When Vancouver constructed its wonderful new library a few years back, local futurist Frank Ogden harrumphed that it was a waste of taxpayers' money because soon everything will be on computer and we'll either read books right off the screen or download what we need. It seems as if logically this must be so. Just as there are no typewriters any more (I have a nearly new IBM Selectric in my basement I can't give away) soon there will be no books.

But if this is true, how come so many new books are on the market each year? And how come there are these huge chains like Waterstone's in Britain, Borders in the United States, and Chapters in Canada? And what makes amazon.com so popular?

I think the experts are wrong just as they were when they said twenty years ago that marketplaces would disappear because we'd all sit at home and order everything—food, clothes, you name it—through a screen in front of us. Though telemarketing became a huge business, Safeway is still here as is Harry Rosen to say nothing of Chapters. This, I think, is because the two things the screen can't give us is a sense of society that comes with the marketplace and the sense of touch and smell that accompanies things like books, food, and clothes.

Of course it will be possible to store all the world's most popular books on a chip so that you can read what you wish off a hand-held computer. But I don't think that's going to happen— at least not for a long time to come. You can't browse through a computer like you can a bookstore. You can't smell the antiquity of a used bookstore in your computer. And no matter what Bill Gates does, a computer is never going to feel like a book does.

I don't think this is old fogey-ism either. I've used computers for writing for nearly twenty years and I'm on the Internet with my own website, which I update daily. No, it's a little like drinking single malt whiskey. It would be no trick at all for drug companies to come up with pills that gave the appropriate buzz of one stiff drink. But you're just not going to have people standing around the canapés, popping a martini pill or a beer pill every half hour or so. There are some things that are ingrained into our souls, and how we take our nourishment, be it for the body or the soul, is one of them. These things won't change. As long as people sip together socially, and shop together socially, there will always be, God be praised, books.

WINSTON CHURCHILL

W ho, of all people in history, has had the most profound effect upon me and my political thinking?

Not even close. Sir Winston Leonard Spencer Churchill, born in the mid-Victorian year of 1874, dying in the midst of the nuclear age and a scant four years before we put a man on the moon.

His personal courage, which I admire even more than I do his way with words, was enormous. At the Munich Conference in 1938 Prime Minister Neville Chamberlain thought he had negotiated "Peace with honour, peace for our time." So did most of the country. Neither the British public nor the media were prepared to hear any criticsm of their prime minister. But Churchill, running straight into the jaws of a much-relieved public opinion, called it "an unmitigated defeat" closing with these marvellous words: "...the whole equilibrium of Europe has been deranged, and the terrible words have for the time being been pronounced against the Western democracies: 'Thou art weighed in the balance and found wanting.' And do not suppose that this is the end. This is only the beginning of the reckoning. This is only the first sip, the first foretaste of a bitter cup which will be proffered to us year by year unless by a supreme recovery of moral health and martial vigour, we arise again and take our stand for freedom as in the olden time." For these words Churchill was pilloried in the press, especially in the *London Times*, denied access to the BBC, and threatened with de-listment by his constituency. In less than a year Britain was at war with Germany, Churchill was thoroughly and absolutely vindicated, and back in Cabinet as First Lord of the Admiralty. Just a year and a half after these prescient words, he was the man entrusted by the entire western world with the task of stopping Hitler.

Churchill is most remembered for his magnificent leadership of Great Britain during the Second World War, especially from June 1940 until June 1941 when Britain stood alone against Nazi tyranny. And he was, probably, the world's last political hero. Improbable as it seems to us, given the leadership we've seen over our adult lives, Churchill did make all the difference in the world. A man of immense personal courage and an unparalleled ability to rouse people with words, he made what seemed like a certain catastrophe into an un-questionable victory.

Let me give you but one example. It's June 18, 1940. France was beaten. The British Expeditionary Force to France had been whipped and had it not been for the miracle evacuation at Dunkirk, the men would have been lost, not just all the arms and armament they were forced to leave behind. The Battle of Britain was about to begin and who but a Churchill would have given Britain a chance against Hitler's Luftwaffe and his mighty Wehrmacht? Who of today's leaders could, after first laying before his people the awesome task ahead, say this: "Let us therefore brace ourselves to our duty, and so bear ourselves that if the British Empire and its Commonwealth last for a thousand years, men will still say 'this was their finest hour.'"

In one sentence Churchill was able to remind the British people of their history, of their legendary and constant bravery, and of their duty. What Briton wouldn't, at that moment, have thought of Henry V at Agincourt, Elizabeth I at Tilbury, Drake with the Armada, and all the deeds that made Britons brothers on Shakespeare's "sceptr'd isle"?

What is forgotten about Churchill—and which has inspired me—was his concern on social issues. Just before the First World War, he and Lloyd George started the welfare state by introducing unemployment insurance, pensions for widows, and labour exchanges for which he was roundly condemned as a "traitor to his class."

Churchill was not only a journalist, a biographer, and the writer of one (not terribly successful) novel, but the Nobel laureate for literature in 1948 for his *History of the Second World War* (Churchill, a great wit, once said "History will be kind to me because I intend to write it.") and also a fine painter.

Yet of all the things Churchill was, he was perhaps at his best as a prophet. He understood that the further you could cast your mind back in history, the further you could see ahead. He was the first man to see Hitler for what he was—a one-off tyrant the likes of which the world had never seen. It was while researching his much-acclaimed biography of his great ancestor, John Churchill, first Duke of Marlborough, that Churchill saw the Nazi brownshirts patrolling the streets, a year before Hitler took power. The instant he returned to England he warned Parliament and the nation of the Nazis and what they intended to do. He was, famously, paid no mind by the leadership of the country inside and outside parliament. He called these years when his warnings about the ambitions of the dictators and their threat to Britain and the world were ignored, "the years the locusts ate."

And his gift for prophecy extended into his later years. In 1946 at Fulton College, Missouri, and at a time when the Soviet Union was still "our great Russian Ally," Churchill reminded his audience, "Last time I saw it all coming and cried aloud to my own countrymen and to the world, but no one paid any attention." But his speech is remembered for these lines "From Stettin in the Baltic to Trieste in the Adriatic, an iron curtain has descended across the continent." Mocked at the time, pilloried in his own land, Churchill once more saw clearly ahead. His "iron curtain" lasted forty-three years.

A few months later, in Zurich, he said this: "I am going to say something that will astonish you. The first step in the re-creation of the European family must be a partnership between France and Germany.... The structure of the United States of Europe, if well and truly built, will be such as to make the material strength of a single state less important." From this was born the Franco-German coal and steel pact and ultimately the European Community.

Before I leave the great man I must tell you that I once met him—sort of. Here's the story.

On the fiftieth anniversary of VE Day in May of 1995, Wendy and I went to London where we met my old pal and former law partner, Stan Winfield. Stan had been in front of Buckingham Palace on that great day fifty years before when the King, the Queen, the two princesses, and Winston Churchill waved to the joyous throng. The evening before the anniversary celebrations, we had a beer or two at our hotel and Stan and I, both being Churchillians, reminisced about the magnificent role played by our hero leading up to the events fifty years before. That discussion started a rather strange series of events.

All three of us went to Buckingham Palace the following day and watched the re-enactment of the scene fifty years before as the Queen, the Queen Mother, and Princess Margaret came out on the balcony. Missing, of course, were King George VI and Winston Churchill. As a squadron of Spitfires and Hurricanes flew past, I said to Stan, resplendent with all his medals, "Wouldn't it be wonderful if God could permit Winnie to appear, just for a few seconds?" After the event, the 250,000 who had jammed the Mall started to disperse and the three of us walked down Buckingham Palace Road to find a pub.

I, nursing a squash injury, sat down for a moment in a door-way and scarcely had I done so when a middle-aged man with two young men in tow came out of the huge crowd and grabbed Stan by the hand and said, "I see you're Canadian. Welcome to London. My name is Winston Churchill and these are my two sons Randolph and Jack." It was indeed Winston Churchill, MP, and grandson of the great man himself. It was a tad eerie. But this wasn't the end of the matter.

To digress briefly, Wendy and I that night went to the monster celebration at Speakers' Corner in Hyde Park near Marble Arch where there was a wonderful show before a crowd estimated at well over 200,000 featuring the Queen and Sweetheart of the Armed Forces, Dame Vera Lynn. We were seated amongst some much older Londoners from the Eastside, which had taken such a pasting in the Blitz. They, complete with picnic baskets and assorted liquid refreshments, were having the time of their lives. When Robert Hardy, of "All Creatures Great and Small" fame and an eminent Churchillian, gave Churchill's speech on VE Day, there occurred a pause and into the deathly silence came the voice of an old lady sitting next to me who, as she raised her clenched fist, shouted "and we stood alone," referring of course to that year between the Junes of 1940 and 1941 when Britain faced the Nazi hordes entirely on their own. I instantly thought of that marvellous cartoon in the *Daily Express* by David Low on the day France fell, showing a British "Tommy" standing on the White Cliffs of Dover, shaking his fist at the approaching Luftwaffe saying "Very well, then, alone." The lady's words, in the silence of that great moment, made the hair on my neck stand up. Shortly thereafter Vera Lynn closed the show with "We'll Meet Again," her great wartime anthem, accompanied by 200,000 of us. There wasn't a dry eye in the house.

Wendy and I went off to Wales for a few days and on the way back agreed we would stay in Stratford for our last night and see a Shakespeare play but that on the way I would show her Blenheim Palace where Winston, a direct descendant of the Duke of Marlborough, was born, as well as the little rain shelter in the gardens where he had proposed to his darling Clementine. After touring Blenheim, we drove a couple of miles to the small churchyard in Bladon where Winston, Clemmie, and other Churchills are buried. On the great man's grave were many bouquets, commemorating VE day and there was one especially touching one, which simply said, "Thank you for freeing our country, from two very grateful Dutch friends."

As we walked out of the churchyard an older woman pushing a stroller with a baby was coming in. I looked at the little chap and said to the lady, "Well, I guess it's true that all babies look like Winston Churchill."

"Well he should," replied the lady, "because his name is Winston Churchill!" No relation, apparently, but the parents had picked Winston as the lad's Christian name.

Perhaps it doesn't seem so spooky in the re-telling but for Wendy and me it seemed as if the great man's ghost had been following us that past several days.

It is strange to note that *Time* Magazine in 1950 declared Churchill to be the man of the half century yet fifty years later called Albert Einstein the man of the twentieth century. Since their accomplishments were contemporary, this is a very difficult circle to square.

I suggest that this is the test—was there one man who, standing alone, made a difference in the struggle to maintain civilization. The clear answer is yes there was—The Right Honourable Sir Winston Leonard Spencer Churchill, KG, O.M., C.H., P.C., MP, soldier, journalist, historian, painter, statesman extraordinaire has now passed through the initial stages of world admiration, through the Monday morning quarterbacking of revisionists, and is now solidly enshrined in the minds of most who think about these things, *Time* Magazine dissenting, the Man of the Century.

How could it be otherwise?

POLITICAL

WHERE, OH WHERE, IS MY PARTY?

I'm looking for something and I'm wondering if anyone out there can help? Perhaps you're looking for the same thing and, like me, are looking in vain. I'm looking, you see, for a political party—a federal political party mainly, but it could be a B.C. provincial party as well. Each of the options available has something of what I'm looking for, but none have enough to get my vote.

In this political party I'm looking only for four things.

First, I'm looking for a party that believes in good fiscal management. Not just good fiscal management after the damage has been done, largely by themselves (like the federal Liberals), but one that has a sound outlook all the time. I am not looking for a party that will never borrow money in an emergency but one that can see the difference between an emergency and short-term political popularity.

I suppose in many ways I'm looking for a government such as we had under Bill Bennett lo those many years ago. I know I would be expected to say this having been a part of his government for five years, but I scarcely feel disqualified on that score. It was a good government that delivered good social services and balanced its budget. It constantly looked for better management in areas where it spent money and looked there first before it simply borrowed money to write cheques.

It's not easy being a government that is fiscally responsible, one that both talks the talk and walks the walk. A fiscally responsible government may not build that bridge or that stretch of highway this year in that politically important constituency.

Bill Bennett refused to put highway construction on a long-term "mortgage" basis (as the NDP did under Mike Harcourt) because he correctly foresaw that this would soon lead to a double-tiered system where there were not only the "mortgage" payments but that governments, yielding to political pressure, would soon want more and more in addition. We would still have the old highways' budget plus that easy pay-as-you-go payment. Fiscal responsibility may even mean postponing a school or a new expensive diagnostic tool in that "swing" constituency you want to win, or perhaps that bridge so long needed. Fiscal responsibility recognizes the obvious (an obviousness lost on the left), that if you have a $36-billion debt, you start your budget process for the year setting aside $2.7 billion for interest payments, many offshore. You also recognize that this is the money that would have built that bridge, or bought that MRI scanner, or made that new school possible.

Second, I'm looking for a party that cares about people. Not a party that pretends it does like the Canadian Alliance, but one that never loses as its philosophical lodestone the fact that people often need help and society at large must provide that help, ungrudgingly. This party, while it believes in the market system, would know that this system has many casualties—especially with globalization—and that some of these casualties were simply never cut out to be part of that system in the first place. I'm looking for a party that understands that, despite anecdotal evidence trotted out by right wingers, most people on social assistance don't want to be there. But I want a party that is really committed to these things, not one that simply writes nice things down on its party mission statement, trots them out at election time, then forgets about them after the election.

In saying this, I must make it clear that I don't want a party so committed to these principles it forgets that the money to be spent on social commitments must be earned. B.C. NDPers are without doubt the best in the world at articulating concerns and fingering social worry beads, but they believe there are corporations out there that, if they only footed their share of the bill, could solve things. They have never understood that money from corporations comes mostly from ordinary taxpayers, be they shareholders (often through pension funds) or consumers. Both groups are at the business end of the cost pass-through initiated by taxes. This gets back to fiscal respons-ibility, but it also means approaching social obligations with a head, not a heart.

There's a paradox here. Throwing money at a problem seldom solves it, but it does solve almost all problems. But money must be carefully withdrawn from the economy so that the golden goose still clucks, even though it might hiss a little as its feathers are extracted, and the money is spent carefully by people who are careful money managers. This is why I think the great health debate about the involvement of private capital misses the point—namely that there is no competition in the public system where there are outcomes against which to measure results. Take hospitals for example. Because they don't compete against each other for patients, it's difficult to gauge performance. The bureaucrats must develop yardsticks by which to make fiscal judgments. It's difficult to believe that these yardsticks are any more realistic than most developed by governments or any other monopoly.

But as with most things, appearances are also very important. Help for the disadvantaged must not be given grudgingly for it is a commitment we as British Columbians and Canadians made long, long ago. It's not right that citizens in need are made to feel like second class citizens by a government which, while offering help, does so grudgingly so as to impress their supporters that they only do so under political duress. So I want a party committed from the heart to helping society's less fortunate, but committed from the head to do it in the most cost-effective way.

Third, I'm looking for a party that has no religion. One that can, for example, debate the question of gay rights on an intellectual and practical basis, not on some obscure verse in Leviticus. There is a decent, logical case to be made for treating gay couples differently than married couples in some respects but it has never been heard because of the tiresome religious prattlings of the Canadian Alliance. In short I suppose I'm looking for a fiscally prudent party that really does care for 100 percent of Canadians, even those whose lifestyles and living arrangements may not be not be fully approved of by the mainstream population.

Last on my list is a party—and this is by no means the least of my concerns—that is philosophically committed to major reforms to our system of government. I put this concern as high as the others because we cannot afford to see our country slip, day by day, into a one-man dictatorship held by a slim thread to democracy through elections every four years or so. We cannot afford to have a country in which all the concern, hence the money, is poured into one region because it threatens secession, and a policy that simply encourages other regions to look down the road to other political arrangements. The reforms I talk about cannot be cosmetic exercises such as more free votes, but real gut-wrenching reforms that go to the very root of our system. That's what the word radical—an honourable political word—means and I'm looking for a radical party.

In looking for a party that's fiscally responsible, that truly cares, and that is dedicated to real reform, I'm not looking for some magic or a miracle. No party or political system for that matter will be anywhere near perfect. I'm simply looking for a party whose philosophical commitment is such that you'll rarely hear the following three utterances:

"I'm in favour of good fiscal management, but..."

"I'm in favour of helping people who need help, however..."

"I'm for reforming the system, yet..."

I think, upon reflection, that I'm looking for something like the late, lamented, B.C. Social Credit party, which was as much about social credit as Jean Chrétien is about Senate reform. It was simply a coalition of all that wasn't of the left and as a coalition was highly successful until Bill Vander Zalm tried to turn it

into a party of the right. I sat in what arguably was the best cabinet British Columbia has ever had, from 1975–79, which had
within it former Liberal and Conserv-ative MLAs and men and
women all across the right-hand side of the political spectrum.
It was a cabinet that knew that Social Credit, as a coalition of
ideas not parties, owed its allegiance to about 60 percent of the
public, which expected it to govern wisely enough to keep the
NDP out and well enough to manage its fiscal and social
responsibilities.

Here is the big problem with the present system and the parties it has spawned. Political parties, quite naturally tailoring
themselves to the system in which they operate, exercise power
from the top down. This has meant that those who wish to par-
ticipate in the process, but are not willing to do so within the
context of blind allegiance to a leader, are so discouraged they
never try or, having tried, leave in disgust. This is why I place
such a high value on "reform" as I search for my party. And
naming a party "Reform" scarcely guarantees its commitment to
it. Witness how Preston Manning, as Leader of the Opposition,
soon started imposing on his members the very discipline his
party's stated principles set out to eliminate.

Is there such a party in B.C. or Canada now?

Frankly no, although the federal Reform party, now the
Canadian Alliance, started out on the right foot and was only
seduced into "going along" as it got closer to power and saw how
the game was played.

Perhaps, after all these years of being involved in politics at
every level, I'm just a dreamer. But doesn't this country also need
some solid dreaming now and then?

THE BIG EVENT THAT
NEVER HAPPENED

On October 26, 1992, a huge event took place that no one ever hears about: the national and Quebec referenda on the Charlottetown Accord. Let me try to explain why this has turned into the event that never happened.

Prime Minister Brian Mulroney saw the Meech Lake Accord fail in June of 1990 when a lone Manitoba MLA, an Indian named Elijah Harper, refused to give the necessary special leave so the Manitoba legislature could debate, and presumably pass, the enabling legislation. To their shame, the Tories generally and Brian Mulroney specifically, laid the blame on then-Premier Clyde Wells of Newfoundland who, upon hearing what happened in Winnipeg, refused to call the question in the Newfoundland House of Assembly. Wells did this because the game was over and he saw no sense in exacerbating further the wounds the Accord had inflicted on Newfoundland. Mulroney picked on Wells because he didn't dare dump all over an Indian—that would have been most incorrect politically.

Mulroney tried again.

Back in August 1986 the premiers, meeting in Edmonton, had unexpectedly handed him a plum. In the absence of their officials they had agreed to postpone all their claims for constitutional changes to those of Quebec. When you think about it, it takes the breath away because what this meant in real terms was that the nine other premiers would see Quebec get everything she wanted including the ability to veto forever more any reforms proposed by other provinces! While Mulroney had been unable to take advantage of this idiocy with the Meech Lake

Accord, thanks to Elijah Harper, in 1992 he took another bite of that plum by appointing former prime minister Joe Clark as the lead in putting together Meech II, or what became known as the Charlottetown Accord. This deal would not only have given Quebec what she wanted plus the ability to veto further changes others may want, but an automatic 25 percent of the seats in the House of Commons no matter what her population ratio was to other provinces.

I have given my take on all this in my book *Canada: Is Anyone Listening?* so I'll content myself by observing that Mulroney called Charlottetown "Meech, Plus! Plus! Plus!"

What happened was this—Brian Mulroney led the Canadian establishment in investing its entire capital in this project. Mulroney started on his famous phone networking and hit every one of Canada's elite, without exception. And they all bought into it. All political parties supported Mulroney. Clyde Wells, whom Mulroney had mercilessly and quite wrongly accused of torpedoing Meech, came on side. Capitalists and union leaders made common cause and the artsy-fartsy set joined in. Even the companions of the Order of Canada jumped into the political arena and supported the "yes" side. And so, for God's sake, did almost the entire media. Indeed Maclean Hunter, in an act of betrayal of journalistic principles that took one's breath away, even registered on the "yes" side! As one of two or three journalists in Canada who steadfastly opposed the accord—the others being Gordon Gibson who wasn't being published at the time, and constitutional expert Mel Smith who had the small right-wing audience of *B.C. Report Magazine*—I was astonished at the lack of professionalism. The closest the media came to addressing the subject was when people like Richard Gwynn wrote articles about that noisy broadcaster in Vancouver, Rafe Mair, who was making all that fuss. No one—politicians, business people, labour leaders, academicians, performers of the arts—was asking any questions. Not even teeny-weeny little questions. Zilch!

When the votes were counted, the result was clear. Six of ten

provinces voted "no," with British Columbia far and away leading the "no's" with 67.9 percent. Even Ontario, though voting
"yes," was almost evenly divided.

The consequences were not as the prime minister and his
lackeys had predicted. The country didn't break into bits. But
the consequences were very substantial for all that. For one
thing, the Conservative party was destroyed less than a year later
in the election of 1993.

Yet no one talks about this watershed referendum. Bill Fox,
Mulroney's chief flack, wrote an excellent book about the
Mulroney years and never mentioned Charlottetown! Not even
a footnote! It's as if it never happened!

As for the media, with the courageous exception of Ian
Haysom, then editor of the *Vancouver Sun*, it was business as
usual the next day. Haysom, to his credit, wrote a piece asking
how the *Vancouver Sun* could so misread the public it served and
promised the paper would do better. It has, though not with
Haysom who was sent packing.

No one tried to analyze the results and see what we might
learn as a nation. It was, due to the utter embarrassment of the
entire national establishment, made into a non-event.

This is a very serious mistake. There is much to learn from
this exercise, not the least of which is the unqualified distrust
ordinary Canadians now have of all set in authority over them.
Across the land there is the whiff of discontent. People are
actively calling into question the institutions of power and those
who run them. The Supreme Court of Canada, the House of
Commons, and, needless to say, the Senate are being questioned.
We have a government from central and eastern Canada while
the official Opposition comes from the western third, mostly
B.C. and Alberta. We are politically split and now have no legitimate national party whereas before 1993 there were three. In
fact, the third largest party in the Commons, the Bloc Québécois
(the official Opposition from 1993–97), is dedicated to the
destruction of the country.

There was the pallid effort of the premiers at their 1997 conference to come up with a constitutional compromise, called the Calgary Accord, but by the time it was watered down by the British Columbia legislature—of which I heartily approved and may have helped in—we were back to a policy of drift.

No leadership. No constituent assembly. No conferences about constitutional matters. Just drift.

In fact, Jean Chrétien—a more destructive force by far than Lucien Bouchard—effectively put an end to any debate on constitutional matters in December 1995 when he caused a Commons' motion to pass that, in effect, gave a constitutional veto to each of Canada's five regions. In doing that he made constitutional discussion moot—after all, if no change is possible, what's the point of talking about it? And make no mistake about it, as long as Quebec and Ontario have vetoes there will never be any reforms to the way we govern ourselves that give equity to provinces outside the centre.

The Charlottetown Accord—the non-event that, though silent, haunts the country as we drift aimlessly along, hoping, like Mr. Micawber, that something might turn up. It likely won't.

WHY THE TORIES DIED

L et me state the theme at the outset: the parlous state of affairs in Canada reflects the collapse—probably permanently—of the Progressive Conservative party although, as I will argue, it will re-emerge as the Canadian Alliance.

At the end of the Second World War, there were three political parties, both in B.C. and Canada: the Liberals, who represented business and rapprochement with Quebec; the Conserv-atives, who represented business and privileged English-speakers; and the CCF, who represented the working man, the downtrodden, and what my father called the "parlour pink," namely, the well-to-do socialist. The lines of division were very clear between these parties. The CCF never came close to power, which is not to say that they didn't exert a considerable influence by forcing other parties to bring in social policy against their will as a safeguard against the socialist hordes. The Liberals made an accommodation with Quebec, which ensured they were in power most of the time. The Conserv-atives represented the Ontario upper crust and were the darlings of the Imperial Order of the Daughters of the Empire (IODE), the Monarchist League, and those who saw French-Canadians as slackers who wouldn't fight for the Empire that so nourished and protected their "habitant" way of life.

The B.C. version of this political coziness was a coalition made up of Tories and Liberals (with the latter the majority force), formed in 1941, ostensibly to show a united patriotic front during wartime. It was nothing of the sort, of course, but simply a contrivance to keep the vote from being split and allowing the CCF (later the NDP) to take power.

It is not safe to assume, because there was for many years (from 1933 until 1952) a Liberal-dominated B.C. government, that dealings with the Liberal government (from 1935 onwards) in Ottawa was all peaches and cream. Indeed the main forces in the B.C. Liberal party, Duff Pattullo, premier, and Gerry McGeer, mayor of Vancouver, were constantly at loggerheads with the government of Mackenzie King and later Louis St. Laurent. In 1952, when a Tory backbencher named William Andrew Cecil Bennett led a ragtag group of disgruntled Tories, funny money freaks, and malcontents to victory under the banner of Social Credit, and then fought constantly with Ottawa for twenty years, it was assumed by those who didn't know better that he represented a new phenomenon. I would argue that Bennett was the logical heir to Pattullo and McGeer.

W.A.C. Bennett came on the scene and consolidated his position as a B.C. "nationalist" (not too strong a term I don't think in retrospect) as great changes were taking place elsewhere. John Diefenbaker rode to power in 1957 on the sentiment, west of the Lakehead, of "fuck you" to the eastern establishment and in the rest of Canada as an antidote to the tiresome, long-term arrogance of the Liberals. Around the same time, Quebec under Jean Lesage rose in its Quiet Revolution with its notions of "maîtres chez nous" (masters in our own house), and the franchise was extended to Indians and Asians. Suddenly there was a different country, different in many ways. The "national" parties no longer controlled the second and third largest provinces and their hold on their counterparts in other provinces declined dramatically. The exception was the NDP, which always considered itself "centrist" and perhaps in part for that reason has never controlled Ottawa.

An interesting manifestation of this erosion of federal party influence occurred in 1979 when B.C. had an election at the same time as the federal one. The leader of the B.C. Tories, and its only MLA, Victor Stephens, demanded that federal Tory leader Joe Clark give him some help, both monetary and vocal.

Mr. Clark declined because he knew that if he became prime minister he would be dealing with Socred premier Bill Bennett, not Stephens.

Then came 1967 and the centenary of Canada's birth. It was a glorious time to be a Canadian. Quarrels were seemingly forgotten and there was a great wellspring of good feeling of various groups of hyphenated Canadians towards one another. It was like the dysfunctional family setting aside all its old grievances as it celebrated together the 100th birthday of its most distinguished member. When the bilingual and bicultural policy of Lester Pearson was confirmed by the immense victory of Pierre Trudeau in 1968, it looked, for just that brief moment, as if we really had something going. Everyone in English-speaking Canada seemed to be learning French while French-immersion classes sprang up in schools right across the country.

By the 1972 federal election, however, the party was over. In Western Canada, the rump Conservative party became the voice of protest as the Liberals barely scraped in with a minority government.

Under Robert Stanfield the Tories prospered. But it wasn't enough to win power, largely because the Trudeau inner circle, including Jim Coutts and Keith Davey, discovered that the Liberals could win with most of Quebec and much of Ontario and the rest of the country could be ignored. This produced electoral victories until 1979, but public opinion in Alberta and British Columbia, especially, smouldered in a distaste for Trudeau and his Liberals that amounted to hatred. The ancient wounds were exacerbated and the fault lines exaggerated.

There was, of course, a brief interregnum in 1979 when Joe Clark fumbled his way in and out of power, but that was followed by nearly five years of Trudeau revenge on the western provinces exemplified by the hated National Energy Policy. The years between 1980 and 1984 hardened the hearts of British Columbians against Ottawa as never before, but there was always the hope the Tories would return.

By this time, however, the national Tories had become, and have remained, two parties: the party of Ontario (and Quebec under native son Brian Mulroney) and its fiscal clients, Atlantic Canada, on the one hand, and the party of "protest" west of the Lakehead.

This is not to say that British Columbia is natural Tory country. It is not. It is naturally Liberal country or, at least, it's middle of the road. What it is, however, is anti-eastern establishment country and during the Trudeau years these sentiments were best represented by the Conservative party and to a lesser degree by the NDP.

In 1983, the hand that held the dagger, Brian Mulroney, had struck it between the shoulder blades of a Joe Clark whose caucus could never really forgive him for having lost a confidence vote and thus power in December 1979. While there was much sympathy for Clark as he was publicly humiliated by Mulroney in the June 1983 Tory leadership convention, there was hope that Mulroney, with some solid support from usually Liberal Quebec, might get rid of the hated Liberals and their despised National Energy Policy. And he did. What British Columbians and most other Canadians had not noticed, or had chosen to ignore, was the Faustian pact Mulroney made with Quebec separatists such as Lucien Bouchard. Mulroney was going to jam it up the Liberals' backside, and that was good enough for us. It didn't occur to us that it would be our backside next.

For while initially it looked like Western Canada was finally going to have a place in the Canadian sun, Mulroney, after winning a huge landslide in 1984, yielded to the central-Canadian half of the party and started the process that culminated in Meech Lake and Charlottetown. This, in turn, led to the election debacle of 1993, which saw the decimation of the Tories and the rise of the Reform party.

(Some point out that British Columbians mustn't have minded Meech Lake too much because they enthusiastically supported Mulroney again in 1988. That ignores two factors.

First, Meech Lake was not understood by most Canadians until 1990 when Newfoundland premier Clyde Wells came on the scene and, second, Mulroney had craftily turned the 1988 election into a single-issue fight over free trade with the United States.)

I have no real sense of what went on in the minds of other Canadian voters on election night 1993 when the Tories were wiped out. However, in B.C. the strong anti-Tory vote, which included throwing out homegrown prime minister Kim Campbell, had much to do with the referendum on the Charlottetown Accord the year previous. British Columbians felt betrayed. Here they had been faithfully supporting the Tories since 1972, because they were the party of protest, yet once in power the Tories turned out to be the party that wanted to preserve the status quo hegemony of central Canada for-ever by changing the constitution. The Faustian pact with the Quebec devil mentioned above was exposed for all to see. The Progressive Conservatives had betrayed our trust just so they could get elected (which after all is what political parties are supposed to do) and had toyed with our affections. Even the redoubtable Senator Pat Carney, forever the strongest voice for B.C. in Ottawa, had supported Charlottetown in the Senate.

It was this enormous sense of betrayal that lofted the Reform party from one member to damn near Official Opposition in 1993 and then to that role in 1997. Of course, the Liberals have been badly beaten in the past so why can't the Tories make a similar comeback?

The two situations are not comparable. For one thing, the Liberals never, not even in the Diefenbaker rout of 1958, came close to the disaster visited upon the Tories in 1993. Moreover, the Liberal party was always strong on the ground in Ontario and Quebec whereas the Conservatives had always depended upon regions outside central Canada for their core support and been essentially non-players in Quebec. The exceptions to this were in 1958, in the first instance, and again in 1984 and 1988 when they jumped on the Diefenbaker and Mulroney bandwagons for a piece of the action. Moreover, the Tories have been unable to find a leader who can lead, returning the leader-ship to the oldest fifty-nine-year-old in the country, Joe Clark, whose main opposition for the top job in the 1999 leadership "race" came from Toronto backroom boy Hugh Segal and a socialist Saskatchewan farmer named David Orchard.

But the main reason for the death of the Tories is a fundamental and unbridgeable crevice that splits the party once you go west of the Lakehead and destroys it once you cross the Rockies. East of that line the notion that Canada is a result of a pact of "two founding nations" is prevalent; west of that line this notion is firmly rejected in favour of seeing the country as ten juridically equal provinces and a federal government. Joe Clark is Charlottetown. He believes in "two founding nations," a "distinct society" designation for Quebec, a Quebec veto, and special representation for Quebec in the House of Commons— indeed in his own words he accepts an asymmetrical Canada. He not only believes this, he actively espouses these views as the salvation of the nation. In British Columbia, voters contemptuously threw out Charlotte-town with the "no" vote at an astronomical 67.9 percent. In fact, it was worse than that. Not a single polling station voted "yes." Moreover, much of the "yes" vote came from people who didn't support Charlottetown but believed Mulroney when he claimed the country would break up the next day if the vote was "no."

But what if the Canadian Alliance party loses its way? Won't the Tories be the beneficiaries? Won't they fill the vacuum?

The answer is no because British Columbians in the main are not natural Tories and have only voted Tory in the past as part of a protest against Ottawa. The Tories are now, as much as the Liberals, the party of central Canada. This is especially true in B.C, Alberta, and, to a lesser extent, in the other prairie provinces. The Canadian Alliance, or something like it, will not die in the far West as long as it appears to represent that region in the longstanding war against Ottawa. The Canadian Alliance likely knows this and must tread a very fine line between making sufficient concessions to the Ontario mindset to gather enough strength east of the Lakehead to gain national power, while retaining its critical western base.

But what if the Canadian Alliance does indeed look like just another Conservative party because of its lust for Ontario votes? B.C. could go back to voting Liberal until another alternative appears. However, the more likely scenario would have western Canadian voters quickly finding another protest party, probably one split off from the Canadian Alliance that, in my view, would be a separatist party in British Columbia and Alberta.

Conservatives haven't gone away—the Conservative party has.

It's the Duty
of the Opposition
to Oppose

"It is the duty of an opposition to oppose." This succinct declaration, one of the basic premises of parliamentary democracy, was uttered by Lord Randolph Churchill 120 years ago, and it's as apt today as it was then. "The government proposes and the opposition opposes" is another definition of parliamentary government in a nutshell.

We don't operate on government by negotiation basis. Nor should we. As with all rules, there are exceptions. There are bills that occasionally, but very occasionally, are passed by Parliament unopposed. Perhaps to erect a statue for a fallen hero or help places ravaged by a great calamity. But even in the most innocent of bills, there is something that can only be discovered and properly thrashed out in the crucible of vigorous debate.

It's instructive to note that during the worst days of the Second World War, during the Blitz and threat of Nazi invasion, the British House of Commons sat as usual and debated as usual. In fact one MP, Emanuel Shinwell, was a constant and very well-informed critic of Churchill's leadership with the uncanny ability to call up facts and figures that caused much squirming on the government front benches. Shinwell was certainly considered a monumental pain in the ass by Churchill, but not for one second was his patriotism called into question. He was simply doing his duty as a member of Parliament.

Churchill, who bore the cares of the entire world on his shoulders for much of the war, was subjected to two motions of non-confidence, which he successfully fought. Again, no one suggests that the supporters of those motions were unpatriotic.

I shudder to think what would happen if we embarked upon a practice of consensus government as they apparently have in the new "near province" of Nunuvut. Politicians are worry enough at the best of times, but when they all agree with one another it is indeed time to count the silverware.

A proposition vigorously tested by the opposition has a very healthy aura to it. If nothing else, close debate often exposes unintended consequences. Those who propose legislation—and here I speak from considerable personal experience—are notoriously bad at noting these unintended consequences just as a writer can edit, re-edit, and edit again and not spot a clanger that is quickly spotted by an editor who has no pride of authorship. And even the best of editors miss a few.

Moreover, it's a rare bill that doesn't have parts of it that are highly offensive to some. In a democracy, those contrary have a right to present their case before the bill becomes law.

But an opposition party nearly always often finds its duty to oppose thwarted by our present system of government. For a variety of reasons, the prime minister exercises dictatorial power in this country and simply cannot, for practical reasons, be held to account. We live in what I call a "soft dictatorship" (more on Canada's "soft dictatorship" on page 165). If the House of Commons were to censure the prime minister, meaning that a majority of the Commons voted against him or his policy, the prime minister would have to resign. This is not a situation any prime minister will permit to happen. However, one of the ways—and perhaps the most effective way—the Commons could hold the prime minister's feet to the fire is through the committee system. Like all parliaments, ours has parliamentary committees covering most key ministries of the government—a finance committee, a foreign affairs committee, a fisheries committee, and so on—which have the power to deal with such issues as they please and can subpoena witnesses including cabinet ministers and even the prime minister himself. Sounds like a pretty effective weapon, doesn't it?

Except it's no weapon at all because the prime minister gets to name the members of the committee from his party, which has a majority on each one, select the chair, and thus set the agenda. Moreover, most government MPs know that any promotion depends upon how they behave. Pretty neat, huh? All the trappings of democracy and checks and balances yet in practice as independent as the members of Saddam Hussein's parliament.

An example from my own province—British Columbia.

In 1999, the Public Accounts Committee in British Columbia, which is chaired by the Opposition in this province, heard from George Morfitt, the auditor general, concerning the "fudge-it-budget" scandal of May 1996. It then decided, as a follow-up, to call Tom Gunton, the NDP civil servant éminence grise, to give evidence before it. Seeing that the committee was getting too close to the bone, then-Premier Glen Clark put an end to it by instructing his members of the committee to adjourn it indefinitely. Then in February of 2000, this very same Public Accounts Committee was investigating the PacifiCats' financial boondoggle and was again getting mighty close to the bone when Glen Clark's successor, Dan Miller, abruptly shut the committee down.

What this means, of course, is that committees simply don't bother asking hard questions because they know that the majority, hand-picked by the leader, will make sure that nothing will be allowed to happen that might embarrass the premier or the cabinet. This applies perhaps even more so to the federal government. Let me give you an example.

The huge healthcare crisis facing Canada has the federal government under attack on many fronts. The Opposition have demanded that this be debated by the Commons Health Committee but its chair has refused, claiming that this is the moment mental healthcare should be debated. Though mental health is clearly of great importance, this is an obvious smokescreen behind which an embarrassed health minister has decided to hide. Thus, with the power to select all people in power of consequence in the country, and with the power to shut down any meaningful dissent in Parliament, Canadian prime ministers and premiers have absolute dictatorial powers. And, as we've seen with Bill Vander Zalm and Glen Clark, no matter how bad it gets, once in power, leaders only leave when they're damned good and ready.

What's this all in aid of? A serious criticism of the system first and foremost, which is dysfunctional, and of opposition parties in Ottawa, especially the Canadian Alliance, formerly the Reform party. From the outset Preston Manning ought to have been on the prime minister's case about the NATO action in Kosovo back in 1999. This wasn't a question of national security, where we must all rally around the flag. This was Canada getting into an undeclared war. Questions abounded. How could Canada, not just a member of the United Nations but a member of the Security Council, sidestep that organization and help Bill Clinton and Tony Blair transform NATO from a purely defensive organization into a highly offensive one? How much say did Canada have in all this? Did the country take steps to try to live up to its duties as a member of the Security Council and persuade members of NATO to reconsider? Did Canada canvass the views of Russia and China and find out not only why they opposed the NATO war but what alternatives they proposed? What sort of commitments were we really in for? What were the objectives and what was the "exit strategy"?

These and countless other questions should have been asked, but they weren't. It doesn't matter whether Manning and all his MPs thought that the Kosovo war was a marvellous idea; he had the duty to oppose it so that all possible considerations would be aired and debated.

The argument that once "our boys" are fighting we should support them is a laudable one, but it became pretty shopworn in the latter years of the Vietnam War when more and more Americans saw the conflict as immoral and unworthy of their country. "Our boys" would be far better served if the Opposition back home was doing its duty and asking whether or not they should be risking their lives in the first place.

This need for close scrutiny and hard debate should extend off the floor of the legislatures and into parliamentary commit-tees, which, as noted, are scarcely ever used in B.C. and are dom-inated by the government party in the House of Commons. One need only look at the Nisga'a Treaty to see what happens when debate is muffled. Neither in the British Columbia legislature nor in the House of Commons was the matter thoroughly aired. There was no Commons committee to look at the Treaty—it was debated from the government side on an emotional basis only. The consequences are sure to be grave indeed as this legislation takes seed and produces many other Nisga'as across the land. The natural instinct of government is to avoid scrutiny and debate of its actions. This is rather like bad science, which accepts the first proposition that seems logical and refuses to test it with the skepticism that is the hallmark of good science. Politics is like science in that uncriticized propositions very often turn out to be catastrophes. Lord Randolph Churchill was right. And more often than not, when his dictum is ignored, the public weal suffers.

They Don't Really Give a Damn, Back There

In 1976 I began my constitutional duties with the British Columbia government. While my formal position was never more than chairman of the Cabinet Constitutional Committee, in the three years that followed I was in effect B.C.'s constitutional minister and as such began to spend a lot of time in Ottawa and Toronto.

Before that time I had been to Toronto only a handful of times and then on business and for just a few days at a stretch. I had, then, the typical native British Columbian's view of Ontario and especially Toronto. Basically it could be called deep dislike bordering on actual hatred.

From childhood on I resented a lot of things about Toronto —in no particular order Sir Ernest MacMillan, the Toronto Conservatory of Music, the CBC, and especially the Happy Gang, George Drew, the Toronto *Globe and Mail* (to which I still add the civic adjective and deservedly so), Foster Hewitt and his son Bill, Bay Street, Canadian banks, the Blue Jays, Lester Pearson, the Maple Leafs especially, and on the list goes. Pearson, a love object for many Canadians, was especially irksome because by his every word and deed he demonstrated that while all provinces might be equal, Ontario was much more equal than others, especially British Columbia.

In all events, I didn't much like Ontario and especially Toronto, even though I had never spent much time there.

When I started visiting Ontario on a regular basis—for a while twice or three times a month—I was told by those knowledgeable sorts that thought the entire wisdom of the country abided in the Toronto *Globe and Mail,* that I would come to see that Ontarians and especially Torontonians really not only loved us but understood us. Well, I spent nearly half a decade putting that proposition to the test.

My contacts throughout this epiphany were Bill Davis— Buttermilk Billy—the premier of Ontario whom I watched at close range through endless conferences as well as his senior staff and political colleagues. I spent hours closeted with Ontario politicians and officials during the run-up to the patriation of the constitution. I may not have gotten to know the man on the street too well, but I sure as hell got to know the people who ran his affairs.

I went to Ontario convinced that central Canadians generally, and Ontarians specifically, knew little of British Columbia and cared even less. Not only did I not change my mind, my suspicions were emphatically confirmed. The bald truth is that Ontarians only consider British Columbia as a source of raw materials and chronic bitchers. They consider B.C. part of a seamless "West," which, of course, it is not. It was only very recently that the Toronto *Globe and Mail,* in its polls, stopped lumping B.C. in with the Prairies as if what was happening in The Pas, Manitoba, bore some relationship with Sooke, British Columbia. Indeed, today Canada's weather report in the Toronto *Globe and Mail* still has four regions, lumping the climate of British Columbia in with Edmonton, Swift Current, and Brandon. This is not, I concede, a big deal. What it is, however, is a clear indication of how Toronto and Ontario see the country.

This, of course, has very important ramifications for Canada. Ontario, with a quarter of the Senate and, through its perennial government caucus, control of the House of Commons, simply cannot understand why B.C. sees Senate reform as a major issue. It is utterly beyond that province's ability (John Nunziata, MP, excepting) to understand why we chafe under a system where 50 percent plus one of the House of Commons has 100 percent of the power. Nunziata is an exception perhaps because he was born and raised in B.C. before moving to Toronto.

Ontarians, generally speaking, see the country as an ongoing saga between Upper Canada and Lower Canada. In their view, solving that debate—or at least keeping it going without Lower Canada dropping out—is what Canada is all about and the other provinces aside from Quebec should simply stay on the sidelines and cheer Ontario on. There isn't the slightest understanding of B.C. history. Ontarians don't know and don't care that, unlike the Prairie provinces, B.C. entered Confederation as a self-governing colony and did so after negotiating as a high contracting party with the five provinces that then made up the country. They don't understand that the deal wasn't to enter a two-party partnership, Quebec on the one hand and the rest led by Ontario on the other. British Columbia would never have accepted this "two founding nation" concept of the country and doesn't for a second accept this notion now.

Much of Canada's recent constitutional history reflects this central Canadian misunderstanding of Canada as seen through the eyes of British Columbians. Meech Lake and the Charlottetown Accord (so called) would have perpetuated central Canadian hegemony over the country through agreements that only faintly sugarcoated that fact. British Columbians by nearly 70 percent demonstrated that they understood this when they voted in the Charlottetown referendum of October 26, 1992.

So Ontario and Quebec don't understand how British Columbia came into being. Because some Quebecers and some Ontarians did indeed move to B.C. in the early years, it is wrongly assumed that the province was populated by some great east-west migration such as occurred in the United States. In fact, B.C. was mostly populated from the south and the west, initially, and thereafter by people who arrived directly from the United Kingdom. The Ontario version of the "typical" Canadian has never lived in British Columbia.

Also much misunderstood is the geography of the province. I well remember attending a constitutional conference in the 1970s where there was a huge wooden map of Canada on the wall. Missing were the Queen Charlotte Islands! When I questioned my hosts, they were amazed that I would be sensitive to the fact that these great islands, which carry so much native and non-native history, should be expunged from our geography. Again, in itself, perhaps no big deal. But cumulatively, little things like this do betray an astonishing ignorance of Canada's third largest province. (In fact, B.C. will overtake Quebec as its second largest about midway through the twenty-first century, which helps explain why Ontario and Quebec especially want preserved forever the status quo.) Central Canadians would do well to fly over B.C. and see how everything—its mountains, rivers, and islands—all flow north-south so they don't see it as such a mystery why British Columbian thinking also goes the same way. Central Canadians would also be well advised to try to understand the notion of Cascadia, which, while it will never become a political reality, may well express British Columbia's economic future.

There is, in my opinion, a grave danger that British Columbia will leave Confederation. It certainly will do so if Quebec goes. But it may go anyway. As political decentralization around the world paradoxically goes hand and hand with economic unions, British Columbia may well find it in its interests to leave Canada and go it alone in NAFTA. This sort of thing doesn't happen by revolution, armed or otherwise. It comes when regions feel unrepresented and uncared for and British Columbia is both of those. It may well be that after another decade or so of chafing under central Canadian absolute rule plus central Canadian indifference, British Columbia will become, what it might have been in the first place but for the threat of American "Manifest Destiny," an independent nation with friendly neighbours to both the east and south.

Then it will no longer be necessary for people in central

Canada to ask, what the hell's the matter with those people out there? What's the matter and what always has been the matter— as I found out for myself—is that "back there" they really *don't* give a damn about us.

THE LEXUS AND THE
OLIVE TREE

G lobalization has got everyone concerned, but it has the "left" in an awful flap. When I say "left" I mean the old-line socialists and those, like labour leaders and others, who still sing from nineteenth-century songbooks. They become apoplectic at the mention of the word. There is a great gnashing of teeth and wringing of hands as they predict the certain and imminent falling of the sky. The trouble is that while the socialist solution never did work, it is now so outdated that modern social democratic parties such as are found in Europe and in the form of New Labour in the U.K. don't even bother to pay lip service to the old notions any more. Socialism died with communism in 1989 when the Berlin Wall came tumbling down. If socialism didn't work when, as in the former Soviet Union, the government introduced it under compulsion and threat of prison and death, how could it possibly work when people were free to oppose its tenets?

Ronald Reagan is credited in many circles with bringing down the old Soviet Union because he money-whipped them. And he did drive the armaments race to new expensive heights, which no doubt tipped the barrel. But the real killer of socialism, whether of the forced or voluntary kind, was the marriage of the Consumer Age to the Communications Age. I'll never forget a visit I made to China back in 1983 and seeing, near the Hong Kong border, hundreds of television aerials pointed at the Hong Kong stations. There was nothing authorities could really do about it. And as the consumer goods and way of life in the West started to turn up on the TV screens in living rooms

behind the Iron Curtain, the difficulties facing communist governments became insurmountable. It was a new theme on the
old First World War song, "How you going to keep 'em down on
the farm, after they've seen Paree?"

With the end of the Cold War and the rise of the Consumer
Age, which now depended not only on manufactured goods but
on services and intellectual property, the pool of capital available
started to look for places to invest. With the arrival of the "chip,"
it was no longer possible for countries to pass currency restric-
tions because with the push of a button money could be and was
whisked off to a safer place. Moreover, if a country did succeed
in forcing its attentions on a pool of capital, other capital
shunned it for future dealings.

There is, of course, this myth based upon umpteen conspira-
cy theories that somewhere some sinister person is controlling all
this capital and using it for wicked purposes. The fact is that capital, like filings to a magnet, is attracted to where it gets the best
and safest deal, and it vanishes into the night when government
pinkies get too close. The old left, wrapping itself uncomfortably
in the flag of nationalism, never ever ready to let an old battle
end or an old battle cry die, talks of withdrawing from NAFTA
and other sillier things. With the enthusiastic support of neo-
nationalists like Mel Hurtig and Maude Barlow as well as the
labour unions, all of whom should know better, a great international wave of revolt against globalization has taken to the
streets, notably of Seattle in November 1999 and Washington
D.C., in April of 2000. This is a revolution without leadership
that simply fears what it sees coming and lashes out in aggressive
self defence. It is not surprising this has happened given the
speed with which globalization has struck and the tardiness of
leadership in the West to level with its people about what it all
means.

There are challenges—lots of them. Not everyone is a winner
in the new global economy, not every country, nor every person.
In fact there are lots of losers. But the compensations have to

come from sound government and personal decisions that recognize the existence of the "electronic herd," as Tom Friedman in his brilliant book *The Lexus and the Olive Tree* calls the new pool of capital. And while the electronic herd can be eased about and directed with guidance, it's not going to disappear. The new world is here and just like the Industrial Revolution in its time, it cannot be stopped. It can be accommodated and dealt with, but it cannot be stopped.

It is the wise country and the wise person who learns about globalization and works out the accommodation necessary to have it a vehicle to prosperity rather than a hearse to the burial park.

But how about the danger to world peace?

Globalization brings with it many benefits to many countries. It is an uncertain pleasure giver because it can withdraw its affections as quickly as it can bestow them. But in the main, countries that benefit will do so very quickly.

On the other hand, there are poor Third World countries that no self-respecting capitalist looking for the biggest bang for the buck will touch. This is a substantial threat to world peace, for leaders of these countries, unable to satisfy the basic needs of their peoples by attracting the necessary capital from the available sources thereof, will try to distract them by pulling at Uncle Sam's beard with a show of military might. And some of these countries have developed or are developing the ability to make big bombs and the ability to deliver them. Two places that come readily to mind are Iraq and North Korea. The United States thinks it has Iraq under its thumb but it doesn't. Tools of mass destruction can be built much more easily than in days gone by and indeed are often available on the open arms market. Moreover, the technology for nuclear weapons, once vouchsafed only to the most learned of nuclear scientists, are now available on the Internet! North Korea is truly a frightening place—its people are starving and its government mad. It has nuclear weapons and, because its obvious targets are so close, the ability to deliver them.

There are other dangerous ramifications. Places like Brazil have huge poverty problems that can be only slightly ameliorated by desecrating the environment. Unless the electronic herd comes and stays in places like Brazil, the economy will take a battering. The only choice left is to ignore environmental concerns to keep people working. Since the herd is not into social issues, unless they make heaps of money, these countries are out of luck.

It is in these areas that governments, especially in developed countries, must develop strategies. It is silly to simply list the complaints one has about the way the world operates and offer solutions that try to undo decisions that cannot be undone. Yes, MAI (Multilateral Agreement on International Trade) was defeated, largely because of the left (though many non-left people were also concerned), and probably rightly so. But something like it must be put in place so that when individual countries have trouble dealing with globalization, collectively nations can exercise influence.

The demonstrations against the World Trade Organization in Seattle and Washington are all the more dangerous in their long-term considerations because they are not for anything but are a reaction *against* the unknown and the apparently unknowable. Much of the blame for this ignorance must be laid at the doorstep of government leaders who, fearing that people will misunderstand, prefer silence to explanations.

A good part of the problem is due to the speed with which globalization and the electronic herd came into our lives and the consequent speed of what is happening around us. Before we knew it, so it seems, phones were ringing everywhere—in theatres, on riverbanks, and in restaurants. A stock transaction that used to take seventy-two hours from order to payment now takes a few seconds. A trip that required time and trouble to arrange is now handled in seconds on the Internet.

Another important aspect is the sudden inability of governments to control their own economies. Whereas in the not-so-distance past governments could control the inflow and outgo of capital, the speed with which online transfers can now be made makes this all but impossible. Governments can't even control the price of their money or, in the jargon of the trade, "peg" the dollar, or pound, or whatever. Take, for example, "Black Wednesday," as the British call it, when on September 16, 1992, New York billionaire George Soros took on the entire British government over its ability to keep the pound within prescribed limits and won, pocketing a cool billion in the process. The world was put on notice that in the battle of governments against capital, capital was the stronger. Indeed in that case, a government was proved powerless to defend its currency against one man—a pretty scary thought.

The main problem with the electronic herd is not when it invests so much as when it moves elsewhere, usually to a friendlier clime. This is where the individual nation is helpless, whereas collectively nations can act.

It's a scary new world out there. The old truths have become passé.

Unpleasant and uncomfortable though it may be to face globalization realistically rather than shout shopworn slogans at it, Canada must do this if it is not only going to survive globalization, but prosper in it.

The left thinks it won a great battle against the World Trade Organization at the "Battle in Seattle" in November 1999 and again in Washington D.C. a couple of months later. But if it was a win, it was only a battle in a much longer war that it's bound to lose. There must be international agreement about globalization, not in the interests of those who have but those who have not. It can no longer be a secret agreement between heads of government free of the crucible of public debate. And it must be an agreement that deals with more than just the shuffling of capital and the protection of businesses. Not for the first, nor, I dare say, the last time have those in power assumed they knew best and that the public, ignoramuses that they are, would be better off not getting involved. Agreement, hard as it may be to achieve, must be reached not just because of the truly worldwide economic effects of globalization but because in a very real and urgent sense, the avoidance of a disastrous war, perhaps even a global war, is at stake.

A VIEW OF
PIERRE TRUDEAU FROM
CLOSE AND AFAR

There is no question Pierre Trudeau was the most interesting and cerebral of our prime ministers. Because he is obviously a great man, the question arises as to whether or not he was a great prime minister. It's not the same question at all. Trudeau was a great polemicist, political philosopher, and writer. And God knows he had charisma. Not only did he demonstrate that in his remarkable campaign in 1968, but to this day he can command a crowd of media just by commenting on some affair of state.

But was he a great Canadian leader?

On the plus side surely is his patriation of the constitution. I personally opposed the Charter of Rights and Freedoms, which was part of the Trudeau package, but he did get the constitution from Westminster to Ottawa where it belongs. There was a price, however. Quebec did not officially sign on even though, according to a unanimous verdict of a full sitting of the Quebec Court of Appeal, as sustained by a unanimous full sitting of the Supreme Court of Canada, Quebec was bound by the new constitution irrespective of whether its government agreed. To this day the bitterness lingers.

What Trudeau did not do, and by temperament was clearly unable to do, was unite the country. He didn't do this because he didn't understand the country outside central Canada. He especially could not understand Alberta and British Columbia despite the fact that his father-in-law James Sinclair was a very powerful B.C. cabinet minister under King and St. Laurent.

Trudeau understood constitutions as pieces of political

science and constitutional law, but he had no concept of how they would be seen by other parts of the nation. He perhaps knew that Ontario didn't speak for the rest of the English-speaking provinces, but he always acted as though it did. The Pepin–Robarts Commis-sion, which travelled the country seeking constitutional feedback, did have one commissioner from British Columbia, Ross Marks, mayor of 100 Mile House, but it still demonstrated Trudeau's concept that Canada was Quebec and Ontario and some other places thrown in. I attended half a dozen or more First Ministers' Conferences, and this was the way Trudeau played the game as chairman. He would defer to Premier Davis of Ontario, deliberately irritate René Lévesque of Quebec, then sit back and smile like a benign father as other provinces, like very small children at the dinner table, tried to make a point.

In fact, Trudeau held the provinces in contempt as did all his ministers. The name of the game was always the put-down. Senior federal officials treated premiers like visiting mayors of small-town Canada and were utterly contemptuous of provincial cabinet ministers.

In 1968 Trudeau was seen, coming as we were out of the centennial celebrations, as the man who would bind the country together. We in "outer Canada" were all excited about learning French. If we weren't going to learn it ourselves, our children were. They were exhilarating times. By 1972 the magic had so evaporated that Trudeau was reduced to a minority prime minister with his representation all but gone west of the Lakehead.

Why did that happen?

Clearly because those in Western Canada, especially those in Alberta and British Columbia, saw the bilingual and bicultural programs of the Trudeau government as "Frenchification" of their provinces. Of course it wasn't seen that way in Ottawa, which missed the point, but it was very much seen that way in places like Vancouver. Looking back, clearly much of what the "Bi & Bi" programs did was catch up for years of keeping

French-Canadians down. But it seemed to most British Columbians that it wasn't in proportion to the numbers but a 50-50 deal with French-Canadians. Everywhere we looked—in the top civil service, in the armed forces, in the federal cabinet, on federal corporations, bodies, and commissions—French-Canadian names were on the top of the letterhead. Whether these assumptions were correct is beside the point. That's the way it was seen. And explanations from Ottawa, when proffered, were by way of haughty suggestion that everyone west of the Lakehead was an anti-French redneck.

The First Ministers' Conference in September 1980, which I attended, really tells the Trudeau story regarding national unity. A senior bureaucrat, Michael Kirby, made a senator as his reward, drafted a cynical document outlining how every provincial initiative was to be thwarted by Trudeau, then had it leaked to René Lévesque. The reason was simple—Trudeau wanted it his way or the highway. It looked very much as if the premiers might actually agree (sans Lévesque, of course) and it would never do for Trudeau to be seen as simply one amongst equals. The country suffered from this arrogance, for later on the Supreme Court of Canada ruled that there had to be "substantial agreement" amongst the provinces and Trudeau did have to go to the hated premiers, constitutional begging bowl in hand. Thus a conference, which many of us saw as the beginnings of a new Canada (such had been the effort put in by all leading up to it), was poisoned from the outset. Trudeau was easily able to make each premier look like a minor parish pump politician as he demonstrated to a willing Ottawa-based media that he and he alone could unite the country.

This, sadly, is Trudeau's legacy. In fairness it must be said that not even the legendary negotiating skills of a Brian Mulroney could have brought Quebec on side in the years René Lévesque was in power. After all, the Quebec government was out and out separatist and made no bones about it. Any deal cut with the nine other provinces and the federal government without the

Quebec government's consent would always be seen as most unreasonable indeed by Quebecers themselves, and there was no deal René Lévesque would ever agree to. It was classic "Catch-22."

One can only speculate on what would have happened if the public humiliation of all the provinces had not taken place at this conference. There could not have been any suggestion of betrayal as René Lévesque pled in 1982. Yet on the evidence I saw, if Trudeau been a leader in September 1980 instead of a self-aggrandizing mischief maker, a deal with nine provinces and the federal government would have been made then, Meech Lake and Charlottetown would have been avoided, and likely so would the 1995 Quebec referendum. Some might argue that Lévesque would have won his referendum in 1980 but I very much doubt it. The "no" vote was 60% and while it might have been lower if patriation had happened with the Parti Québécois government's consent, I believe it still would have failed.

Of course this is speculation, but what is not speculation is what happened. Trudeau in 1980 and afterwards utterly destroyed the sense of subsuming regional ambitions for the national good amongst provincial governments so essential to maintaining national cohesion. Worse than that, he destroyed it amongst the populations of the various provinces so that when Brian Mulroney tried to repair the damage with Meech Lake, Charlottetown, and beyond, the public—increasing in anger as one went west—rejected his plans. Granted they were bad plans, and Mulroney was playing to his own political timetable, but the anger was planted by Trudeau, not Mulroney.

But surely in addition to his impact for good or ill on national unity, Pierre Trudeau will be judged on his other permanent monument, the Charter of Rights and Freedoms. For it was, unquestionably, "his baby."

In 1982, when Pierre Trudeau patriated the Canadian Constitution from Britain to Canada, he demanded that a Charter of Rights and Freedoms be entrenched in the new

Constitution so that it could not, realistically, ever be changed. This was a marked departure from our system and practice for it took the protection of rights, individual and collective, away from Parliament (which had its own Bill of Rights) and gave it to an unelected body, the Supreme Court of Canada. This concept was not without its opponents, notably premiers Sterling Lyon of Manitoba, a Tory, Allan Blakeney, a Saskatchewan NDPer, and Bill Bennett, a Socred. The opponents to the Charter were not, as painted by the proponents, against people getting rights. As Allan Blakeney put it, "When my rights are challenged, I want to go to my MP, not my lawyer." What these three premiers foresaw was a gigantic transfer of power from Parliament, which, for all its faults, is elected, to a court, which is not. What the proponents didn't dream of, we, the opponents, knew—the Court would interpret their way to supreme power in the country.

Alex Macdonald, a former attorney general in B.C., has written an excellent little book called *Outrage, Canada's Justice System on Trial,* which demonstrates just how, by using the Charter, the Supreme Court of Canada has drained away so many police powers the criminal courts have become like law school "moot courts" where fine legal nitpicking can count for far more than truth and justice. Macdonald, to his credit, also admitted that when I, as minister responsible for constitutional matters, raised the government's objections to the Charter, he and his fellow NDP MLAs of the day paid no mind. Few others did either.

The Supreme Court, which once confined itself to straightening out miscarriages of justice, both criminal and civil, and arbitrating constitutional disputes, has now become a glorified department of social work. It now has become very Americanized in its approach, ignoring common sense for a "right" driven agenda. Let me give but one example. Back in 1956 in a case called Kuruma vs. the Queen, the Privy Council decided that even if evidence was illegally obtained, if it was otherwise admissible it would be admitted. In this case a suspected Mau Mau terrorist in Kenya was jumped by police officers who found some rounds of ammunition in his trousers, then a capital offence. The gist of their lordships' reasoning was that while Kuruma might well have an action in assault against the police, he was nevertheless caught with the goods. By that time, the United States courts, following the individual rights route dictated by their Bill of Rights, had gone quite the other route, holding that evidence obtained illegally was a "poisoned tree" calling justice into disrepute, and was thus inadmissible no matter how compelling it was.

Canada had a choice. Not bound any more by the British Privy Council and certainly not bound by American decisions, it could go either way. This Supreme Court, in granting Charter rights hither, thither, and yon, has rejected illegally obtained evidence even, indeed often, when the only illegality was the police officer's failure to give an appropriate warning or to give it quickly enough. We have even reached the stage—I'm not joking—where in Canada drunkenness has been used as a defence to drunk driving because the accused was too drunk to understand the police officer's warning!

Fortunately, thanks to the premiers' stubbornness in 1982, the Charter of Rights and Freedoms has a "notwithstanding" clause whereby Parliament and the legislatures can, by specifically saying so, pass legislation "notwithstanding" its provisions. Quebec did this with its language laws, but otherwise legislators have been reluctant to face the political heat from the "higher purpose" persons, mostly of the left, who would set their collective hair on fire were such to happen.

I predict that the temptation will increasingly be for provinces to use the "notwithstanding" clause to protect provincial legislative powers and will thus become a divisive factor. Indeed the better view may be that, far from uniting Canadians, Pierre Trudeau's Charter will do much to divide them. Today, the opinion is widely held that the legislative function has been largely taken over by the Supreme Court of Canada just as premiers

Lyon, Blakeney, and Bennett predicted it would be in 1980.

Pierre Trudeau is the man who established the prime min-
isterial monarchy and put the finishing touches on the castration
of the MPs. It was he who presided over establishing the Prime
Minister's Office, peopled by nameless and faceless unelected
insiders as the focal point for the exercise of power. Parliament,
already hobbled by its inability to control its own affairs because
the prime minister has taken it over, finds itself competing with
the Supreme Court of Canada for the right to legislate. It must
reassert itself and soon. It should start with the criminal law and
so-called "poisoned tree" evidence. Though not strictly a Charter
case, Parliament is going to have to deal with Delgamuukw
before it sends us all into the poor house. For, as predicted by
those who opposed the Charter from the outset, Canada is fast
becoming governed by the unelected and unaccountable.

In assessing Trudeau it must also be remembered that it was
he who launched the country on its descent into debt. Until his
reign the rule was a surplus, the exception a small deficit. Under
him the deficits soared. The last surplus until Paul Martin in
1999 was John Turner's budget in 1974. Trudeau was disdainful
of those who thought that fiscal responsibility went with public
office. It was not that one could discern any special agenda that
required the government to take the national debt to astronomical heights. It just seemed that, as far as Trudeau was concerned,
buying votes with taxpayer's money was a legitimate means to the
end of having him in power—and to him, any alternative to that
was unthinkable.

I watched Pierre Trudeau close up for five years. I first met
him at a small luncheon in 1976 in Victoria, hosted by Premier
Bill Bennett and attended by half a dozen B.C. cabinet ministers.
I was struck by his smallness—most people thought that
between him and Joe Clark, the latter was the runt. That was
undoubtedly so in terms of personality but not in height. I was
also surprised at what seemed to be shyness although I later
learned that this was a façade covering a steely resolve to yield

nothing of his thinking until it suited him. He was Jesuitical in argument and the best example I saw of this was over the Charter when the objection was raised that it would truncate parliament. Trudeau listened to all the weighty legal arguments, backed with constitutional precedents, then shrugged and asked "Don't you want Canadians to have rights?"

Pierre Trudeau ran First Ministers' meetings like a strong-willed teacher might preside over a high school council meeting. Those he didn't intimidate, he simply ignored as too unimportant to notice. At the end, he would sum up for the record, which summing up was always a brilliant summation of what he thought, but which bore little relationship to what was said by others.

Trudeau governed through force of a personality that cowed people, especially his caucus. There was no love there but an abject admission that they were no match for him individually or collectively. He was a man not to be argued with and no one did.

Was Pierre Trudeau a great Canadian?

A great man?

Give him a B+.

A great Canadian?

A D at best.

YIPPEE! A NEW
GOVERNOR GENERAL!

The cry of delight rolls across the land as another political hack gets the $100,000 per year, plus expenses, all tax-free sinecure of governor general. Be it Jeanne Sauvé, Ray Hnatyshyn, or Adrienne Clarkson, you can be sure that a lifetime's fidelity to the party in power was the first consideration in Her Majesty's gracious appointment of the prime minister's latest selection for Government House. Not only is the incumbent, Adrienne Clarkson, Liberal down to her pink underdrawers, she even spouted the party line in accepting as the "first woman not from one of the two founding nations." You can bet from this CBC groupie this was no slip of the tongue.

What a glorious but lost opportunity Jean Chrétien had to cover a number of bases long waiting to be covered. He could have appointed, for the first time, a British Columbian who also has a physical disability and, most of all, is loved by all as a courageous man who has done more for Canada than we can ever acknowledge. Just how the hell Rick Hansen could lose out to a central Canadian Establishment star, from two perspectives—the CBC and her Liberal connections—is quite beyond me. But, come to think of it, why would Chrétien do anything to please the unwashed out here? The Liberal Party hasn't given a damn about B.C. for decades.

Of course what must surprise one most is that Chrétien didn't take care of that perpetual thorn in his side, Conrad Black. Permit me to explain.

Now for those who have been on Mars for the past few years, let me introduce Conrad Black, also known as "Tubby," and his chatelaine, Barbara Amiel, aka "Babs." Mr. Black until recently owned almost all the papers that matter in Canada—no, the Toronto *Globe and Mail* doesn't matter, at least not any more—and he also owns the *Telegraph*, the second largest of Britain's broadsheets. Even though he has sold his Canadian papers he will control the *National Post* for five more years. Indeed Mr. Black is very big in Blighty, so big that he demanded from Tony Blair, and got, a peerage—at least he nearly did. It was no problem for Blair, but it was for the man Black torments daily, the Right Honourable Jean Chrétien. Black is a Conservative, you see, and Chrétien is a Liberal. Chrétien also happens to be, in Black's mind, a lousy prime minister and one who uses the old political pork barrel even more effectively than did Black's great good friend Brian Mulroney. From the Black Bully Pulpit, otherwise known as the *National Post*, Black has made Chrétien's life miserable. Not only has Black exposed all the evils of the Liberal government, of which there is an abundance, he has demonstrated that Chrétien has been a very generous donator of public funds to his own riding. In turn, Chrétien, through the use of an ancient parliamentary ruling against Canadians accepting foreign titles, advised the Queen that turning Mr. Black and Babs into Lord and Lady was just not on in the realm of Canada. Black sued Chrétien but, alas, got second prize and stepped up his journalistic attack on the prime minister.

It came to pass that as all this was going on, Chrétien found himself in need of a governor general. And his eye, directed by the political lice that attach themselves to prime ministers of late, came to rest on a Chinese-Canadian, an oh-so-faithful-establishment-type lady by the name of Adrienne Clarkson. Indeed, by a "liberal" extension of the term she could even be regarded as a refugee, which made it all the better.

So here's the scene. While the said Ms. Clarkson was plying her trade as an oh-so-faithful-establishment-type contributor to the Canadian Broadcasting Corporation and Mr. Black was seeking his British barony, Chrétien was mulling over his choice for the next governor general. He had a problem with Clarkson though. Her live-in boyfriend, a leftish but oh-so-establishment writer named John Ralston Saul, was, well, a live-in boyfriend. Could Clarkson fix up that little potential blot on the national escutcheon? Turned out she could. There were two quick ceremonies, a plighting of troth with Mr. Saul and a swearing in, and before we knew it, we had a brand-new, oh-so-establishment, Liberal-type governor general, a new "first gentleman," and the world unfolded as the Liberal world should.

But what have Tubby and Babs got to do with all this?

Why, what a glorious chance to buy off a tormentor at no cost to the political capital of either himself or the Liberal party of Canada. It was a cinch. Enthusiastically support His Tubship's quest for a title and, indeed, suggest that it should be at least an earldom. Then have the new earl and his countess become the next governor general and chatelaine of Canada! In a trice you've tamed the *Post* and its able reporting tormentor Andrew MacIntosh, easily the best political reporter in Canada, thus avoiding all the nasty political mumblings that threaten your re-election. Plus, Canada would now have its very own titled head of its oh-so-establishment oligarchy. Such a deal! And he blew it!

This brings into focus the whole notion of what a governor general actually is and does. At one time they were usually chinless aristocrats from Blighty no one knew quite what to do with. By 1935 we'd managed to snag a distinguished Scottish author, John Buchan who went under the alias Lord Tweedsmuir, who was followed by another chinless aristocrat, the Earl of Athlone, followed by a war hero, Viscount Alexander. The system was working well. Not only did we have the colonial trappings, we had a real live member of the British upper classes to guide us. Just listening to those toffee noses with their plummy accents talk without moving their lips was an inspiration to us all. Why they gave us a nice park, Stanley, two nice cups, Stanley again and Grey, plus schools and hospitals all across the land that otherwise would have been named after real Canadians. Then, just as the system was working so well, the Liberals changed the rules and in 1952 established the present process by appointing a rich member of the establishment, a Liberal, of course, in Vincent Massey. Since then the line of political hacks is almost unbroken, the obvious exception being Georges Vanier. Since the job does nothing useful, why bother?

I suppose the answer is that there are ceremonial roles in running a country and we must have someone to play them. Moreover, there may again come a time—the last was seventy-three years ago—when we need a Queen's representative to make constitutional decisions. Very well, I propose this as the way to keep politics out of it. Let the Queen nominate three utterly useless nobles—they could be from the ordinary nobility but more desirable would be candidates from amongst the minor royals (if there are any not in trouble for snorting cocaine). We could then let the companions of the Order of Canada, who think themselves the equivalent of nobility anyway, and who are most skilled indeed at recommending political hacks since they and the governor general decide who will get Order of Canada awards, make the selection. And let's make it for life so we can really get to love the silly old fart who gets it.

There is, of course, another alternative. We could actually—this may shock more sensitive eyes out there—elect the governor general. Admittedly this democracy bit is not in accordance with our usual practice, but why not give it a try? Now there is a real problem with electing people—they may take their victory to be a mandate to actually do something. And candidates may make promises such as nicer rose beds at Government House or a change in manufacture of the vice-regal limousine. There could be no end to this sort of thing.

But in reality, it just might work. It has, for example, in Ireland. The incumbent, the second female in a row, actually comes from Northern Ireland and is very popular. Her predecessor, Mary Robinson—a Catholic married to a Protestant—did a magnificent job in spite of her lack of powers and lack of mandate to do anything. But this would never do, would it? If we let the people decide, how could Liberal prime ministers pay off debts or get inconvenient colleagues out of the way? After all, the prime minister is fortunate if he has a half a dozen senate seats to hand out during his term and besides, though they don't do much, senators are expected to do something.

I suppose it's a bit of a paradox. Nobody cares much about the governor general but on the other hand, why can't one of our kids get it sometimes instead of it always going to a member of the ruling political aristocracy?

Not to worry, I suppose. Just good old Canadian tradition at work. Sift amongst the political ashes and find a Liberal whose appointment will thrill the chattering classes and make the eastern establishment feel warm all over.

And Adrienne Clarkson does fit that bill admirably.

ETHNICITY IS HERE
TO STAY

It is the great hope here in Canada that the separatist feeling in Quebec will go away. That time will take care of it. It is a hope that will never be fulfilled.

There are some things that never go away—at least not for hundreds of years.

Look at Ireland. The grievances are centuries old going back to the first Norman invasion in the eleventh century. The wrongs inflicted on the Irish are real, if somewhat exaggerated from time to time, whether it was Sir Walter Raleigh in the sixteenth century, Cromwell in the seventeenth, or the Coercion Laws of the nineteenth. They continue in the consciousness of north and south (especially in the north)—and the United Kingdom—and they show no signs of going away.

The plantations of people under Elizabeth I, Cromwell, and William III are represented to this day by dedicated loyal subjects of Her Majesty who simply won't countenance union with the republic to the south. The northern Protestant, who is no more an ardent churchgoer than his Catholic neighbours, nevertheless marks his Protestantism every time any question of nationalism comes up.

We are now in the twenty-first century, yet Ireland is no closer to a real solution than she was a hundred years ago. There is an appetite for a modus vivendi, but no appetite on either side for all solutions thus far put forward. Moreover, by 2010 at the latest the Catholics will outnumber the Protestants in the North, which will intensify the desire of nationalists for union with Eire.

Ireland is a remarkable island—remarkable for its people, its scenery, and its history. Mackenzie King once said that some nations have too much history while Canada has too much geography. Ireland is one of those countries with too much history.

But Ireland, like the Middle East, like the Balkans, and perhaps like Quebec, presents ethnic realities that, lamentably, have stood the test of centuries. So often we try to make complete and final judgments where none are possible. And to do that, we decide that some things are bad, some are good, some people are right, and others are wrong. Life is not that simple.

Often, geography plays its part. Ireland as a country is first of all very affected by the fact that it's an island. While it has been subjected to many migrations, since the arrival of the Celts there has never been mass migration as that which swept over Asia, Europe, and the Americas. Irish people in "modern times" have been invaded and have seen massive transplants but, unhappily, no absorption of those who arrived as Protest-ants in a Catholic land after the Reformation. Catholic Ireland did not have a Reformation as did the rest of Europe, and as the Anglican Ascendancy came over Dublin Castle, to all the other areas of disagreement was added religious persecution.

As an island immediately to the west of England, it has long had great strategic value to the British and that's caused lots of grief. As a result Ireland, all of Ireland, has rarely been without political and economic strife to say nothing of military violence.

While the Irish see the British as foreign invaders with little understanding of the Irish—which is true—the British see the Irish as a constant threat to their security—which is also true. The Battle of the Boyne in 1692, the Uprising and French Invasion of 1798, and the denial of ports to the British in the Second World War clearly demonstrate this.

What has happened, of course, is that Ireland, like Canada, has developed into two solitudes—one, mostly but by no means exclusively in the south and Catholic; the other, mostly but not exclusively in the north and Protestant. This religious gulf is a very deep one and has manifested itself in the strange political situation in the north where parties don't divide along political lines but religious ones. This has brought extremists directly into the political pool and one immediately thinks of the Reverend Ian Paisley, a man whose anti-Catholicism is sometimes so outrageous as to border on the humorous.

Paisley sees any reunification of Ireland as the imposition of Catholic rule, yet before one simply writes him off as a crank it's wise to look to Ireland's most literate spokesman, Conor Cruise O'Brien, himself born Catholic and who says that until fairly recent times there was something in what Paisley says. There was, according to O'Brien, an appetite in Dublin for bringing the north into a Catholic Ireland where many laws (abortion, divorce, and the like) were dictated by the church in Rome. This has clearly changed in the past twenty-five years, though the influence of Rome is still strong. It is certainly stronger than the Ulster Unionists who, in a province where all political parties are secular, would prefer to be dominated by Protestantism.

Paisley is certainly correct to deduce that as the peace process brings the two Irelands closer and closer together with greater and greater integration, it follows that sooner or later Ireland will be one, no doubt ruled from Dublin. What Paisley doesn't accept, of course, is that if the steps are gradual and peaceful, such reunification may be more in the interests of the north than the south.

In fact, the terrible tragedies of recent years have raised the level of utter disgust felt by both sides. The 1999 murder of a Catholic lawyer in the north by a Protestant militant group showed that the propensity to violence remains on both sides though it is also true that the people are less and less willing to turn a blind eye to those in their midst who practice violence as a political tool.

I travel to Ireland on a yearly basis now and I would never hesitate to do so for safety reasons. But I sense a different feeling in Ireland. I believe it will take as many centuries for the problem to go away as it did for it to develop in the first place, but there is strong change in the air, a strong sense in both communities—especially in the north—that this strife is unacceptable. Too many families have been affected by tragedy. When you have calamities like Omagh in 1999 and Enniskillen a few years before, every soul is seared by the horror.

St. Patrick is the patron saint of all of Ireland and as we celebrate his day every year, we might also celebrate the tremendous changes that have come over that land in the past few years. Personally, I feel genuine and reasonable hope that these changes will continue and, to paraphrase Lord Durham's famous one-liner about Canada, that these "two warring nations within a single bosom" will slowly but surely come together in peace.

Now look across the Irish Sea. Scotland became part of the United Kingdom in 1603 and joined Britain formally in 1707, yet the appetite for a separate Scotland has never gone away. No matter that Scotland has more MPs in Westminster than its numbers warrant. Forget the fact that it has more money spent on it per capita than England or Wales. The desire to separate, be it a form of Home Rule or complete independence, is deep in the soul of the Scots.

The devolution of powers to the new Scottish parliament and the Welsh assembly should be of interest to Canadians for several reasons. For one thing it shows, as I commented earlier, that ethnicity dies very hard indeed. It's only a few years from the 300th anniversary of the Union of Scotland and England and the abolition of the Scottish parliament, yet the urge for independence remains. So those who think alienation in Canada will go away are, of course, not reading human nature very well—especially when that alienation is based upon ethnicity.

In Scotland we also have the chance to see how proportional representation works. Will the various regions of Scotland—and there are many—find not having their own special member upsetting? After all, there is a world of difference between a Shetlander and a Hebridean, between a Highlander, a Midlothian, and a Border Scot. What proportional representation has

done, however, is make it very difficult for the Scottish Nationalist party, which favours full independence, to gain power. That's
because it rarely produces a majority. The downside of that is if
the Scottish Nationalist party ever did get to power, independence would follow quickly.

Canadians may find it interesting to see how devolution of
powers to a region works in practice. It's true that the provinces
have distinct and substantial powers, but these don't include
making their own money or developing a full legal system all
their own.

Is it just possible that the looser federation in the United
Kingdom will work? If it does, it won't be without problems, not
the least of which will be the question of why the Scots MPs
should be able to vote on matters that only concern England
and Wales.

Wales has been united with England since 1536 in a formal
way and for a couple of centuries before that in reality, yet the
sense of Welshness remains strong and the language still much
spoken.

In the case of Ireland, Scotland, and Wales, there have been
conscious and deliberate efforts to assimilate. The native
languages have been discouraged. There has been much inter-
marriage. Yet the nationalism remains.

What lessons are there for Canada?

The decision not to assimilate Quebecers into a society dominated by Anglos was prompted by reality. In 1760, after the
conquest, Quebec was peopled almost exclusively by the French.
Britain was having plenty enough trouble with the Thirteen
Colonies below and didn't need a lot of trouble in its new colony.
In fact the guaranties of language, laws, and culture in 1774, far
from being acts of generosity, were directly related to the unrest
in the rest of British North America.

Until 1960, English-speaking Canada was able to "control"
Quebec because of the huge influence of the Roman Catholic
Church and the innate conservatism of the French-Canadian.

The English controlled the business community and there was sort of an understanding of what everyone's place was. This changed after the Quiet Revolution of Jean Lesage and it's been quite a different ballgame ever since.

The popularity of the separatist notion will wax and wane. The 1980 referendum, in spite of the curious wording of the question posed by the separatist Parti Québécois government of René Lévesque, was about 50-50 amongst French-speaking Quebecers in favour of separation. In 1995 it was more than 60 percent. Clearly, the notion of a separate Quebec has a very strong base, with deep roots amongst its French speakers. Just as clearly, unpopular though it made him, Jacques Parizeau was quite right to blame the "Anglos" and "ethnics" for costing the separatists the referendum of 1995 and it's upon this bloc of votes the federalists must rely.

But there is this cause for deep-seated worry. The Anglophone numbers are slipping. More than that, the Parti Québécois is making a conscious effort to create amongst non-French-speaking Quebecers a sense of Quebecness. This doesn't mean that the 20 percent non-French will suddenly convert to separatism, but it does mean that it won't bother them quite as much. What the separatists hope is that Quebec will gain some important converts and that, like Ireland, from the non-French community will arise a Wolfe Tone, a Charles Stewart Parnell, an Arthur Griffith, or an Erskine Childers, Irish Protestant "nationalists" all.

I am always amazed when politicians and ordinary Canadians alike think that because a referendum is "won," the problem has gone away. It has not. It has just been adjourned.

And it's silly to talk about how high the "winning" percentage must be, for if 50 percent plus one decide to separate, a new dynamic will take over and there will be no stopping the separatists. What we must know and understand is that ethnicity is part of Quebec—and part of Canada as a whole—and that that is not going away. It is an integral part of the great experiment that is Canada.

Unhappily for those who want this great Canadian experiment to continue and to work, the precedent of separation referenda, now firmly established, means that while separatists can lose again and again, those who want the country to stay together can't ever afford to lose one.

WHO WILL BELL THE MEDIA CAT?

T he proposed merger of America Online (AOL) and Time Warner ought to give lovers of press freedom everywhere, very much including Canadians, cause for alarm if not downright fright. Globalization has very much watered down the national character of news dissemination so while the hugeness of the AOL/Time Warner merger catches our attention, concentration of media power in Canada has already happened and there is no reason to believe that this concentration will not, in the near future, be dominated by foreign interests. We like to kid ourselves about foreign ownership—that great Canadian company Seagram has its headquarters in New York and is in all material respects American as was that great British Columbian company Macmillan Bloedel.

It's not that there is a media monopoly in the making either here or in the United States—at least not in the traditional sense—but that we will have all our news delivered to us by the right wing. The worry is not monopoly but domination by like-minded capitalists. At the end of the day there'll be perhaps half a dozen people in the world who will control the media market. And all of them with be of the far right. When I say controlled, I mean tightly controlled.

Canadians have lots of cause to finger their worry beads and finger them quickly. There are, for all intents and purposes, two controllers of our print media: Ken Thomson and now that he has bought out Conrad Black, Izzy Asper. Though they're both getting out of community papers, the power remains with them. And though Asper is a big "L" Liberal, neither owner could be considered wide-eyed liberals, much less of the left. More important, neither could for a moment be considered impartial.

But, they say more than just a trifle disingenuously, they never tell their editors, columnists, or reporters what to write. In fact this is not true. Where the influence of the media barons is sinister is in what they suppress—sometimes subtly, sometimes not so subtly.

Greg Felton is a fine young writer for the *Vancouver Courier*, which I was privileged to write for for three years. In 1999 Felton wrote a column taking the state of Israel to task for its foot-dragging on the peace process, a position taken probably by 60 percent or more of Israelis judging from the 1999 election. There wasn't an anti-Semitic suggestion in the entire article—it simply criticized, in a well-documented article, Israel policy. The *Courier's* principal, though I understand not majority, shareholder is Hollinger (i.e., Conrad Black), which is run by David Radler, a Jew who once published the *Jerusalem Post*, turning it from a moderately left-wing paper to one on the far right. Radler raised hell with the *Courier*. Felton had to retract his statements and to this day both he and the *Courier* are on probation and not publishing any editorial content critical of Israel.

This is disgraceful. For my part, I wouldn't even silence a man like Doug Collins, who is a disagreeable anti-Semite who deliberately baits Jews. What he writes is despicable rubbish, but rubbish in print and on the air is the insurance premium we pay for freedom of speech and of the press. No, what Radler did was utterly wrong. It might be permissible in the sense that the man who owns the press can say what is printed by it, but it violates the code by which journalists are supposed to be governed.

But, apart from these kinds of blatant examples, we can in essence take the moguls at their word when they say that they never interfere with what is written in their newspapers. The fact is they don't have to. They hire the editors—and they don't hire editors who disagree with them. Any editor who does disagree in any material way for any length of time is outta there. And this works its way down the line. Columnists who incur, or would likely incur, the wrath of the big boy are either fired or reassigned. Is this simply an irresponsible statement without any evidentiary backing? Consider this from my own experience. Back in the '90s, the *Vancouver Sun* employed three columnists, the brothers Stephen and Mark Hume and the late freelancer John Massey. They all wrote critically about a proposal by Alcan to further restrict the flow of the Nechako River and thus place even further risk on the sockeye salmon that pass through that river on their way to spawn. While it seemed obvious that the project, called the Kemano Completion Project by Alcan, and Kemano II by many others, seemed to be a done deal, the criticism of the Humes and Massey were printed by the *Sun*.

By 1994, serious opposition to this project had started and I think I can say, however immodestly, that I played a major role through my radio program on CKNW98 in Vancouver. As the opposition grew, Massey was dropped on the spurious grounds that the paper was reviewing its policy on freelance writers. Then, as if by magic, both the Hume brothers were assigned to special projects or told not to write about Kemano II any more. The editorial pages of the *Sun* began to reflect a pro-Alcan message although, more to the point, as the issue heated up to the point where the B.C. government terminated the project, the editorial pages of both the *Sun* and the *Province* (both Southam papers) were deathly silent. Here was a billion-dollar project, under such huge and ever-growing criticism that the government was forced to kill the project, and the two major papers in Vancouver were acting as if they'd never heard of the case! It's rather like the Sherlock Holmes' mystery where it was the absence of a dog barking that caught the master detective's attention. So it is with the media.

I used to write a column for the late *Financial Post* and in one submission roundly criticized the Toronto *Globe and Mail.* The column was spiked. Not that the *Financial Post* was in any way

corporately connected to the Thomson-owned *Globe and Mail*—
it wasn't. I was simply told by my editor that it was against the
newspaper's policy to be critical of another paper! Think about
that for a moment. Not only will a Canadian paper not be critical of its own ownership or permit criticism of itself in its own
paper, it won't permit any unkindness about a rival!

Given this sort of situation, where no media mogul will permit criticism either of themselves or a rival, is this not, in effect,
a monopoly at least as harmful as the one John D. Rockefeller's
Standard Oil of New Jersey in the early years of the last century?
Or that of Microsoft?

What about in radio—is there management censorship there?
If there is, I've seen little evidence of it. But might it not be said
that I am a safe pair of hands for the right-wing owners of my
station?

The evidence would contradict that notion. I pilloried the
Vander Zalm government from the start, and the station management, especially John Plul, the vice-president for public affairs,
was solidly for Vander Zalm and even gave him his own program
to counteract mine. Yet I got two new contracts during this time.

I badmouthed the Vancouver Canucks' management when
they and CKNW were roughly owned by the same interests,
and while I did have a row with the program director, I stood
my ground and again, shortly thereafter, signed another and
better contract.

I did as much as anyone to bring Alcan's Kemano II project
to its knees, scarcely making any friends in the business community, which advertises at my station, for doing so and won
the prestigious Michener Award for my efforts—and signed a
new and better contract.

But having said that, I worry for the future. As long as Frank
Griffiths Sr. was alive and overseeing the WIC Corporation that
owned CKNW, we all knew there would be no interference
with the views expressed by on-air performers. CKNW is now
owned by a large national company who may well tolerate me

for the short time I have left to ply my trade, but I would argue that I'm already a lone maverick. Will it be in the corporate interests of Shaw Cable to keep on the air a man who flails away daily at the "establishment," be it political or corporate?

Only time will tell. And the point is they and they alone will decide what is free speech, what is good journalism, and what is fair play.

We must do something. Yet no matter what solutions are suggested, the devil is always in the details. The Tom Kent Commission of the 1970s identified the problem—and it is worse today—but could not come up with a solution that made the media fair without the government, in whose interest it is to have a temperate media, getting involved. And if the government has the power to discipline the press, it has the right to control it. (One of the outgrowths of the Kent Commission was the Press Council. A more useless disciplinary body it would be hard to find if it weren't for the benchers of the Law Society and the College of Physicians and Surgeons.)

Those who favour some government involvement should hearken back to the 1930s and that haven and spawner of free speech, the United Kingdom. Winston Churchill was warning with deadly accuracy about the dangers of Hitler and Nazi Germany. He was denied the right to broadcast by the BBC whose boss, John Reith, simply did not agree with Churchill and supported the appeasement policy of Neville Chamberlain. Since in those days all radio was controlled by the government, this effectively denied Churchill a broadcast voice and no doubt contributed to Britain's unpreparedness. (Geoffrey Damson, editor of the *Times,* even tried to get Churchill delisted by his constituency.)

Once governments get the power to make "responsible" decisions, whatever those in power think is responsible will, to the exclusion of contrary views, be permitted. Perhaps the simplest answer is the best. Pass a statute making it unlawful for there to be too great a concentration of media power, then let the judges decide what is or is not too much. It's true that judges too are appointed by governments, but there are a lot of them and there is a strong tradition of independence.

Perhaps there is no other solution than to have a government fund available for "untraditional" media. Even then, what is legitimately untraditional and what is not will be decided by the very people providing the funding.

It is a thorny problem indeed and, in the absence of any workable solution, media consumers must at least aware that while they may not always get the media proprietors' views, they can be damned sure they'll not hear anything with which they profoundly disagree.

And if you need proof of that statement, hearken back to the 1992 referendum on Charlottetown wherein every single media outlet swung in behind the "Yes" side, with Maclean-Hunter even registering for the "Yes" side! Can you believe it? Surely it takes the breath away to recall that the owner of Canada's self-proclaimed national magazine and the then-publisher of the *Financial Post*, a very influential national newspaper, actually registered on one side of the biggest political question since Confederation! But every other chain was also on side and every editorial in every rag in the country, to the bitter end (and oh how bitter it was for them!), supported the "Yes" side. In British Columbia, the *Sun, Province,* and the Toronto *Globe and Mail* went on and on about the benefits of this wonderful constitutional deal. The *Vancouver Sun* singled me out, labelling me "Dr. No" probably because the only other voices against the deal were British Columbians Gordon Gibson, Brian Kieran, and Mel Smith who had very limited coverage, while I had perhaps 125,000 daily listeners on CKNW. When all the media agree on anything, the Canadian public is entitled to smell a rat—a very big odoriferous rat.

The media is run by a very few for that very few and there is very little if any journalism left in Canada. And that is ultimately fatal for any country that professes to be democratic.

THE CASE FOR LEADERS

W inston Churchill, in my mind the clear winner for Man of the 20th Century, was a heavy drinker and suffered from depression. Franklin Roosevelt was a womanizer and guilty of clear deception of his Congress and the people. Mackenzie King talked to his dead mother and later to his departed dog. Gladstone walked the streets of London "saving" prostitutes. Lloyd George had a problem keeping his fly done up. Yet all these men led their countries during very difficult times and are seen as "great men."

How well could Churchill have governed Britain when they stood alone against Hitler and the Nazis had he faced media scrums demanding to know how many brandies he'd had the night before, or for breakfast that day, for that matter, and when he'd had an episode of his "black dog," as he called his depression?

How well would Lloyd George have done in the First World War if the media were on his case for bedding down his secretary. And could Franklin Roosevelt have guided America into the Second World War and then help win it if the media had been hammering him for being less than candid about his plans to get the country into that war and for having lusty affairs in spite of heavy iron leg braces?

There seems to be a dividing line, coincidental with and probably running from the rise of television, between immorality in leaders either being not reported or not mattering, or both, and any sort of immoral conduct being a very big deal indeed. It's not that the media in the past did not pillory leaders. The cartoons of British leaders in the 1800s were brutal. The sainted George Washington was viciously libeled on more than one occasion and Jefferson was accused of fathering children by a slave (recently proved true by DNA testing showing that even the most salacious of journalism might be accurate!). There also seems to have been a period in time, roughly from the turn of the 20th century until about 1968 when "muckraking" was frowned upon—though it was there—and the public simply extracted no political penalty when politicians strayed from the moral fold. I select 1968 because John Kennedy and Lyndon Johnson, the former for bedtime activities, the latter for that plus shady business dealings, got away with murder while Johnson's successor, Nixon, was brought down by lying about some political shenanigans.

Britain, a nation of eccentrics, seemed to tolerate politicians' immorality until quite recently. The United States has had quite a history of salacious and less than honourable goings-on at the top but in recent years we find them interwoven with constitutional issues of some importance. What jumps out from modern times is that the public has gone from either not knowing or not caring much, or both, about their leader's private conduct and his moral behaviour to caring so much that a little oral sex and some fibbing nearly brought down the president of the United States.

(It's curious to note that the only other president than Clinton to face impeachment was Andrew Johnson whose personal life made that of, say, Lyndon Johnson, look like a choirboy's yet his sin was a pretty thin case of breaching the constitution by thwarting an act of Congress.)

Undoubtedly the advent of television, and its concentration on presidential peccadilloes, has been a major factor in the problems faced by recent American presidents. But I see this as coinciding with the long, and as yet unresolved, struggle between the president and the Congress.

The government of the United States, as we all know, is made up of three branches: the executive, the legislative, and the judicial. The theory is that the checks and balances this system provides avoid a dictatorship and ensure democracy. And, I would argue, it does just this, though, of course, imperfectly.

Since the beginning of the United States at the great Constitutional Conference in Philadelphia in 1787, the struggle for power has been ongoing, especially between the president and Congress though the third branch, the Supreme Court, got into the act when FDR tried to pack it in the '30s. I only mention this latter point because to Congress, this was a blatant example of a president grabbing power he wasn't entitled to.

The modern struggle started with Abraham Lincoln who, quite unconstitutionally, however defensibly, brought forth the Abolition of Slavery Proclamation. Then there was Theodore Roosevelt who, on his own, fomented a revolution in Colombia so that the "independent" country of Panama could be created and his beloved Panama Canal built. This strengthening presidency, with a lapse for Taft, continued under Woodrow Wilson who was elected in 1916 with the promise to keep the "boys" out of foreign wars, then promptly took his country into the First World War.

After the war, Congress fought back. With three weak Republican presidents following upon Wilson's failure to get the Versailles Treaty past the Senate, the balance of power returned to Congress.

In the Dirty Thirties and during the Second World War with Franklin Roosevelt, the power swung dramatically back to the White House where it stayed until Richard Nixon's resignation.

Looking back through Canadians eyes, Franklin Roosevelt didn't seem all that dictatorial. After all, his main efforts to defeat or ameliorate the effects of the Depression passed Congress, albeit a supportive one. If there was any trouble with checks and balances, it came from the Supreme Court, which struck down so much of his legislation. Moreover, Roosevelt had a devil of a time getting help to Britain before Pearl Harbour in December 1941, but the fact is he did circumvent

Congress to get the "old destroyers for bases" deal through in 1940. He also managed to arm-wrestle "Lend-Lease" whereby Britain got arms "on loan" through Congress.

The fact is that at the same time Canada was seeing its Parliament lose power to the prime minister (as discussed elsewhere) just as the reign of Churchill, capped off by Margaret Thatcher, heralded the dramatic move of power from Parliament to Downing Street.

Harry S Truman, to the surprise of most, was arguably a stronger president than Roosevelt. He got the United States into the Korean conflict without the required congressional approval and was lucky that the United Nations backed him up. By the time Richard Nixon arrived on the scene, Congress had come to see the presidency as having usurped much of the power given it by the Constitution. Indeed, the fall of Nixon, though preventable had he simply owned up to Watergate instead of stonewalling, was as much a matter of Congress taking on a wounded president for its own reasons as it was a concern for integrity in government, a commodity not known for its abundance in Congress.

I think it can be successfully argued that with Richard Nixon, the personal conduct of a president was seen as a weapon Congress could use in its never-ending struggle to tame the White House. The latest example of this was, of course, the impeachment proceedings against Bill Clinton.

Looking back from the vantage point of a few years, the whole Monica Lewinsky affair was pretty silly stuff. Granted that Bill Clinton was a moral leper and Nixon a big-time liar, but since when did morality count in the White House? Clinton wasn't elected to be chief Eagle Scout but president of the United States. After all, Grover Cleveland was a noted womanizer who fathered at least one child with a woman other than his wife. Indeed the common jingle of his day was "Ma, Ma, where is Pa...Gone to the White House, ha, ha, ha." Warren Harding was, if anything, worse than Cleveland. Franklin Roosevelt showed stunning agility from a wheelchair as he pursued Lucy Rutherfurd and "Missy" LeHand. In fact, Lucy Rutherfurd was with FDR when he died at Warm Springs, Georgia, in April 1945. Dwight Eisenhower had a mistress during the war and his successor, John Kennedy, had a dizzying sex life going all the way from movie stars to a girlfriend of a mobster. And if the standard of presidential probity was that set by Lyndon Johnson, Bill Clinton looks like a choirboy.

Granted that the foregoing trysts did not always get publicity, but that proves the point I think. These things were never considered important enough by the media to exploit. But, it's said, the real problem with Bill Clinton was not that he did the things that he did, but that he lied. I suppose that's a big deal if we have come to expect our leaders to tell the truth. But surely it's not overly cynical to say that we expect no such thing from political leadership. Indeed, we expect quite the opposite and given a chance, we'll vote for someone who lies to make things sound good over one who does not. As I've already mentioned, Woodrow Wilson and Franklin Roosevelt told whoppers to their electorates.

Still, following Senator Gary Hart's fall from grace (you may remember that leading up to the 1984 presidential election, he ran off with a woman not his wife on a boat called *Monkey Business*) you would have thought Clinton would have learned the perils of the unfastened zipper. He clearly did not. And, as millions of philandering husbands and wives have done before him, when caught out he lied through his teeth. Strange, when you think about it, that a population that has the morals of an alley cat in heat—the American public—elected representatives who nearly brought the leader of the free world down for receiving oral sex. However, this much must be said for the apparently hypocritical American voter —at the mid-term elections in 1998, in the midst of the impeachment proceedings, they voted in support of Clinton's party in greater numbers than they had in 1994. (From all this there does come something of value.

Never again will a young swain have to explain to his girlfriend what a blow job is.)

What, then, is it we expect of our leaders in these presumably more enlightened times?

Of course we expect them to lead. We want them to make the sort of governmental decisions that guide our country through the good times and the bad. We sometimes demand fiscal responsibility—though in fact elections prove over and over again that we just love being bribed with our own money.

We expect our leaders not only to give us sound domestic policies, with an eye on the public purse, but also to guide us in our relations with the world. What we don't expect them to be, evidently, is human. Moreover, I would argue, we don't expect them to do the very things many of their fellow countrymen do on a regular basis.

People fornicate and do so with great regularity. Magazines sell millions of copies each month to people who want to not only read about others' fornications but also learn how to do it better themselves. People also lie and cheat on a regular basis. They cheat on their spouses—the divorce statistics don't come close to telling us the full extent of extracurricular loving—and they lie on their income taxes or welfare applications. Employers lie to their shareholders and their workers; and workers' unions lie to employers and their members who lie right back. In fact, if someone tells the truth when a lie would have achieved something important for them, they're seen as fools.

When you think about it, society would break down into chaos if we all spoke the truth at all times. "Do you like my new dress, dear?" "No, it makes you look like a cheap tart." "Would you like to come to my house for dinner, dear employee of mine?" "I can't think of anything in this world I want to do less." "Did you, Mr. Taxpayer, honestly eat all those dinners and drink all those drinks with clients in pursuit of business?" "Of course I didn't—it's all just part of a tax fiddle."

These very same people demand that presidents don't get

extramarital blow jobs, that they don't in[...]
tricks, and that no matter what the circum[...]
complete unvarnished truth in every matter an[...]

Is it the media's fault? I suppose one could m[...]
ment and indeed I have made it. On reflection, h[...]
media anything more than an extension of the publi[...]
There was, you may recall some years ago, the toe-sucki[...]
dent with "Fergie," the Duchess of York, and her then[...]
adviser and boyfriend. The *Sun* sold out three editions show[...]
the pictures and I, in London at the time, strictly in the interest[...]
of science, I assure you, couldn't get a copy. The broadsheets like
the *Times* and the *Telegraph* clucked their tongues at the lack of
professionalism in the *Sun*, a tab. Yet I ask again—who's to
blame here? The paper that satisfied the huge public appetite? Or
the public appetite?

I maintain that as long as there is a public prepared to lap up
scandalous and salacious gossip, backed up by enterprising
photographers, there will in a free society be someone to publish.

The public has, of course, changed. In 1939, it was considered the cutting edge of profanity for Clark Gable to say to
Vivien Leigh, "Frankly, Scarlett, I don't give a damn." Married
couples on their honeymoon were shown the next morning
wearing pyjamas and sleeping in twin beds! In 1936, it was considered quite appropriate for the editors of all British newspapers
to censor, by consent, the story of how the King was bedding,
and wished to marry, a twice-divorced American. How today's
royals must yearn for those less enlightened times when the great
actress Mrs. Patrick Campbell said that she didn't care how or
where they did "it," as long as they didn't "frighten the horses."

Undoubtedly TV made the difference. Its immediacy meant
that the competition to tell all became white-hot. Uncontrolled
by leagues of decency and fuelled by the energy of the sexy '60s,
there were few if any constraints on either language or activities.
Movies, to compete, had to outdo TV. The newspapers, facing
redundancy because they no longer were the first word on any

than that being seen on
'70s not because Nixon
d before that. It went
ferred their leaders to
e transgressions went

residential blow jobs
tial candidates. No
a bit of censorship
inet minister who
his favourite foot-
ms irrelevant, in
10 do so, however, we must
ns of free speech and freedom of the press.
to me at any rate, is far too high a price to pay for the comfort of those in authority or otherwise prominent on the public
stage.

There is another way, of course. The public could rise as one
and demand an end to all reporting of salacious goings on by
people of prominence. Needless to say, that's not likely to happen. We are content to be hypocrites instead and cluck our
tongues at the tabloids like the *Sun* while enthusiastically lapping
up everything they print.

WHY CANADIANS ARE
PISSED OFF WITH THEIR
"SOFT DICTATORSHIP"

W ho's your MP and who cares? And why do voters feel dis-
connected from their government?

Because we bloody well are.

Take the case of Dr. Edward (Ted) McWhinney, QC, a noted
expert in international and constitutional law and the Liberal
MP for Vancouver Quadra.

In 1999, the Honourable Jane Stewart, then Indian Affairs
minister, introduced Bill C-49, extending the powers of native
bands to expropriate land. McWhinney's constituents, very much
including native women, opposed this bill so Dr. McWhinney
spoke out against it and lobbied the minister as hard as he could.
She refused to bend, and how do you suppose this intrepid
fighter, Ted McWhinney, voted when the matter came before the
House of Commons? Why, in favour of course.

Why? Because so-called "responsible government," we're told
in school, is so terrific it is in fact an utter and abject failure that
should be tossed out and replaced with a republican system just
as soon as we can.

The theory of "responsible government" is this: the prime
minister and his cabinet are selected from the elected Parliament
so, if they displease that same Parliament, it will vote a lack of
confidence in them and they will be obliged to resign. In reality,
the very opposite is the case and, instead of legislators holding
the prime minister and his cabinet's feet to the fire, it's the prime
minister who tells MPs precisely what they must and must not
do—at all times.

How does the prime minister accomplish this?

To begin with, he appoints and dismisses cabinet ministers and since those who are in want to stay there and those who are out want desperately to get there, the PM has complete control over the behaviour of caucus.

The prime minister makes and unmakes parliamentary secretaries—a stepping stone to cabinet—who get a lot more pay, lots of perks, and get to go on neat trips with the minister to whom they are responsible.

Parliamentary committees, by which parliament is supposed to restrain the executive, are controlled by the prime minister appointing his own MPs, who constitute the majority, and the chairs. It is not surprising that committees thereafter do nothing to embarrass the prime minister or his government.

The final and most powerful weapon the prime minister has at his disposal is the one no one talks about—because they don't have to. The prime minister can, if he wishes, withhold his signature on a candidate's official papers meaning the candidate no longer has the official support of the party.

The bottom line is this—legislators under our system are about as powerful as blind newborn kittens. Those voters who claim that they vote for the candidate not the party clearly don't understand how our system works.

Canada is a democracy for twelve hours every four years or so when we get to select a new bunch of eunuchs to represent us in the chamber of eunuchs that is run as Iron Curtain prime ministers used to run their parliaments—with an iron fist. In Canada, legislators do as they are told.

What should be done?

Why not permit, when, say, a third of the Commons demands it, a secret ballot? Why, it is said, that would be the death knell of parliamentary democracy as we know it! We must see just how our MP votes! But we already know now how the buggers will vote because party discipline forces them to vote as they're told.

Add to the secret ballot the rule that a government need only resign on a budget matter or a motion of confidence, add to that an amendment to the Elections Act removing the right of a party leader to approve a candidate, and power is returned to the MPs and thence to the people who elect them.

Some political leaders are trying to come to grips with this problem in a superficial way. They talk, for example, of "free votes." But in doing so they hope you don't notice that while the vote may be declared "free," the leaders will still pay careful attention to how their caucus votes.

While we're talking about sacred precepts that we're told by political leaders we shouldn't countenance changing, let me propose that we rid ourselves of a couple of others.

Our legislative chambers, with the exception of Manitoba's, are designed so that the government, sitting on the right of the Speaker, faces the opposition, sitting to the left. These benches, going back to more boisterous times, are two sword-lengths apart.

Winston Churchill once said, "First we shape our buildings, thereafter they shape us." And, as in so many things, he was dead right. Our chamber is designed for the maximum comfort of the government and the greatest possible amount of opposition hostility.

Why not do as most democracies do and have the chamber horseshoe-shaped, with the government, that is, the cabinet, seated across the front of the horseshoe and the Speaker's dais behind and above them? Then why not have the other members seated alphabetically according to constituency so there aren't homogeneous cheering sections?

If you combined these structural reforms with the potential for a secret ballot, surely you would bring into the chamber, for the very first time, actual debate. We call the goings-on in the House debate, but it's nothing of the sort. There can be no debate when the outcome is beyond doubt from the very start. All that goes on now is a certain amount of bluster for the media and a few lines for the record, but little else. The government is always going to win, so it's all form and no substance.

Let's talk for a moment about minority governments. Canadians have been bred and wed to the notion that minority governments are a "bad thing." We want stability and efficiency. We usually get neither. Worse, to the extent we get stability it's the stability of autocracy. But the greatest power on earth, the USA, really has a minority government by virtue of its division of powers. Theirs is a system of compromise even when one party controls both the White House and Congress. Because of the division of powers, and the fact that this substantially reduces the presence of party discipline, all legislation is born from a debate character-ized by great skepticism. The system also ensures that all regions have a say. Since the government doesn't fall on an adverse vote, congressmen and women are much freer to vote the wishes of their constituents or the dictates of their conscience.

The president still has great power: while Congress grants the budget, the president and his cabinet spend it. Moreover, he has many ways he can bring political pressure to bear on Congress as a whole and individual members of it. Then there is the unassess-able power of the president's prestige. He can often go over the top of Congress to the people.

Presidents can often make or break congressmen while presi-dential candidates often rely upon the support of congressmen in key states. In fact a mayor can make a difference as Richard Daley in Chicago did in 1960 for John F. Kennedy.

But can one look back over the history of the United States and say that its ability to govern itself has been choked off by the checks and balances in its system? It has, after all, become the world's greatest power. And it has worked its way through enor-mous social and economic problems.

To make my point about minority governments or systems where power is divided, I'll look at two fairly recent B.C. gov-ernment policies that have proved to be abject failures.

In 1978, the Bill Bennett government put many of its Crown corporations under one public company in the private sector and gave every British Columbian five shares as the new company went on the market. I was in the government at the time and in fact in the early stages was responsible for the departments whose cooperation was necessary to make BCRIC, as the company was called, work. From the beginning this idea had very little debate in cabinet, none in the government caucus, and, of course, who cared about the opposition? One of the many reasons BCRIC failed was that holdings were restricted so that "outsiders" could not get control, which in effect meant no one was really in charge and the free market forces were constrained. But my point is this—could this scheme have been nullified, or made viable, if all MLAs had been free to assess it, amend it perhaps, or even tube it?

Fast forward to the late '90s and the Fastcat ferries project, which was the plaything of the premier of the day, Glen Clark, just as BCRIC was the plaything of Bill Bennett. One need only read the scathing report on this project by B.C.'s auditor general George Morfitt to see just how dreadful the process was. There was no business plan and no real control of costs on what was a brand-new technology. The notion that this scheme would enable B.C. shipbuilding to go on the world stage was never tested by any sort of "due diligence" or market surveys. At a time when B.C. hospitals and the entire health system was screaming for money, the Glen Clark government spent about half a billion dollars on a scheme that was a financial and practical catastrophe. Would this have been permitted to happen if the premier had not only had to get this past his own cabinet and caucus but also past a legislature that was not bound by ironclad party discipline and could have strangled the policy at birth?

There is, of course, another way to guarantee a minority government and that is to change to proportional representation (PR) where parties elect MPs off a list of candidates prepared by the party with each party getting as many MPs as their percentage of the popular vote warrants—the method used in almost every democratic country in the world. This is a hugely complex problem. In New Zealand, where they have had a partial PR system, electing one half their MPs off a "list" and the other half by our method of "first past the post" and the jury is still out.

What is certain is that our system doesn't work and is getting worse as more and more power is centred in the prime minister's office. What I propose is this: while we examine by nationwide debate what we should do about the way we govern ourselves we can, without any constitutional amendment, take away the prime minister's power to control votes in the Commons and his power to keep out party nominations that displease him. The Commons could then retrieve its power to appoint its own committees and its chairs. We could even go further and do as the British Labour party does—give to the caucus the right to say who goes into cabinet leaving the prime minister the power to allocate portfolios.

My proposals will scarcely provide perfection—but then, as Churchill said, "Democracy is the worst form of government except for all the others which have, from time to time, been tried." But what I suggest will restore power and dignity to the MP and thus the electorate, and I submit that this would be a very good start.

DIRECT DEMOCRACY

L et's talk about the competing theories of democratic government. The more liberal view is that we should all get a direct
say in what happens. The conservative view was espoused by
Edmund Burke more than two hundred years ago when he said,
"Your representative owes you not only his labour but his judgment and he betrays you instead of serving you if he sacrifices
the latter for your opinion." In a strange irony, it is the Liberal
government that resists all efforts to move to direct democracy,
while it is the conservative Canadian Alliance that espouses it.

The Burke dictum has been the hallmark of the British parliamentary system and might be called the pure representative
system. Because you the voter are so removed from the seat of
power and the means by which to make an intelligent decision,
best that someone who you trust and once voted for do your
thinking for you. Indeed it's hard to see how governing could be
done in Burke's time, the eighteenth century, if it weren't government by representation. Bristol, which Burke represented, was a
hard three days by coach from Westminster and one could hardly
expect an MP to spend most of his time on horseback checking
out matters of state with his constituents—especially since in
those days the franchise was a very narrow one indeed and could
always be expected to support their man in Parliament.

The swing away from the Burkean theory started with the
American Revolution where, in theory at least, power came from
the people who had means, through Congress, to hold the executive's feet to the fire. But even there the matter of participatory
democracy was slow to come, and its highest expression was still

incomplete at best. It's true that in many states the referendum or initiative is common, but nowhere in the great republic has this form of government come anywhere near to replacing representative democracy. And this is no referendum or initiative process in place at the national level. Even so, many Canadians—especially supporters of the Canadian Alliance—look to the American system not as it really is but how they imagine it to be with considerable envy. The essential Burke dogma no longer has the factual support it had in 1778.

Transportation has dramatically improved so that every constituency in Canada, bar those in the Far North, is reachable in a few hours. They have been instantly reachable by radio and telephone for decades, and now that the fax and e-mail are here, we have an abundance—some would say a superabundance—of travel and information possibilities. No longer can the MP say to his constituency, "I had to vote without getting your approval because there wasn't time to inform you." Indeed, the way government leaks and the media picks up those leaks, the voter often has the vital information before the politician.

Have we then reached the stage where MPs should consult their voters on every issue, perhaps by a huge electronic poll where the voter simply presses a "yes" or "no" button when asked for an opinion?

Some Alliance MPs would have us believe that this is not only possible but desirable. One Vancouver Alliance MP, Ted White, uses the "straw poll" to get his constituents views on a wide range of subjects and is very popular for it.

Let me tell you where I stand and why.

I believe that there are some matters that clearly lend themselves to the referendum or plebiscite. (I use the word referendum because that's the popular word, though governments can use a public vote as binding or merely advisory.) Matters for referenda ought to have two things going for them. They should be issues for which there is a clear yes/no option and they should pertain to the social contract, for want of a better phrase.

In our history, provinces have used the referendum to decide whether or not they would be "dry" or "wet." This met the standards because the use of alcohol is clearly a societal issue and is capable of a simple yes/no. Often, although in recent years it has become passe, it was fashionable for municipalities to seek money bylaws for parks, schools, swimming pools and the like. These matters went to the root of how the community lived, were clearly yes/no questions, and were thus appropriate for the referendum question. Referenda have also been held in the past concerning Sunday activities—again, matters that, however mildly, went to the question of how we live with one another.

It gets a bit more difficult when the issue is more complicated. For example, in 1944 the government of Mackenzie King, having promised that no Canadians would be drafted into the army, wanted to change its mind. So it held a nationwide referendum. This conscription question was so complicated and convoluted that one wag asked why they simply didn't ask "What language do you speak?" since the question really broke down to Quebec versus the rest of the country. But the question asked at that referendum could have been simply put if the convoluter of all convoluters, Mackenzie King, had been so minded. He could simply have asked, "Are you in favour of compulsory service as long as the war lasts?"

The difficulty of an issue doesn't necessarily mean it can't be framed in a yes/no question. Both Meech Lake (which didn't go to referendum) and the so-called Charlottetown Accord, which did, were complicated. But so is a general election where a great number of issues, often complex, are answered yes or no by the voter. The point with Charlottetown was that it sent to the root of how Canadians were to be governed, and it was thus most appropriate that Canadians be given the chance to review the issues and vote. And that is the point with "gut issues"—even though the matters may be complex and intricate, given sufficient time the public can inform itself and govern itself accordingly.

The trouble with Charlottetown, and the reason that the establishment still won't even acknowledge that it happened, is that the establishment thought it was a no-brainer—that the Canadian public would do what its betters told them to do. It's for this same reason that the public of British Columbia was not given a vote on the Nisga'a deal, which very clearly went to the root of the social contract as admitted by then-Premier Clark. The trouble was that Clark and the federal government knew that if Nisga'a was put to a referendum, there was a very good chance it would fail. I believe it would have. As with Charlottetown, the support for the initiative at the beginning was strong, but, again like Charlottetown, the longer people looked at the deal and thought about it the more reluctant they were to give their approval. In fact, I would argue that the notion of a referendum on any serious matter is now dead because of Charlottetown except on constitutional matters where many provinces, including B.C., have laws requiring public approval before a change can be made.

But back to the philosophical. How far should we go with the referendum notion? We surely can't expect to have a vote on everything a government does if only because even with voting machines in every living room there are just too many rules, regulations, and policies happening every hour of every day for instant referenda to make any real sense. But what about on major matters such as sending Canadian troops to Kosovo or the Persian Gulf? Should we have voting machines in every constituency where a registered voter, after appropriate identification, could press a button that would let Ottawa know what he or she thought? Why not? The technology is mere child's play.

Would only a few take the time to vote? Well, about 35 percent of Canadian voters don't bother to vote in general elections, and we don't use that as an excuse to abolish them.

Would it mean government by the elite, meaning those who had the ability and too the time to inform themselves?

Probably, but so what? Anyone who has been in government as I have knows that the emperor truly has no clothes. The leaders of our country and province aren't particularly wise people. They certainly aren't omniscient. Does anyone really suggest that most of our MPs are so intellectually superior to the masses who elect them that their opinions are perforce superior?

There would not likely be the appetite there for "direct democracy" if "representative democracy" really did represent the people, but it clearly doesn't. In fact, under our system, representatives can't even represent their own opinions much less those of the voters unless those opinions accord with those of the leader.

Edmund Burke wasn't wrong—but he wasn't right either. Times have changed and the voter is easier to communicate with and better informed. The real problem with the referendum is that politicians only like them under two circumstances—when the referendum will confirm their judgment or when it will get them off the hook. What they can't stomach is the referendum that might cause them to lose face—and votes. It has not been lost on the political elite that the Charlottetown Referendum of October 26, 1992, caused the wipeout of the Tories the following year.

Direct democracy? Or representative democracy? Or, as we now have it, sham democracy? Those are the issues facing Canadians in the twenty-first century.

THE SUPREME COURT—
BEYOND THE PALE?

Since the arrival of Pierre Trudeau's Charter of Rights and Freedoms in 1982, it isn't only Parliament that rules us. In ever increasing doses we're seeing the courts do the equivalent of legislating. Because of this, I regard the subject of the Supreme Court of Canada as a very serious one and the manner appointments are made to it as something all Canadians ought to seriously study. (For more on this, see Pierre Trudeau.)

The Supreme Court of Canada is extremely powerful, yet it hasn't even got a bare thread of democracy connecting it to the people. As it stands now, it is the prime minister alone who says who will go on the court though the pretext is that the minister of justice makes the decision. It can and does strike down federal legislation and, while the power is a negative one, this makes the Supreme Court of Canada a more powerful legislator than any government and its decisions, apart from using the "notwithstanding clause," unappealable.

Let's examine the powers of the Supreme Court.

For starters, it decides on issues between the federal government and provinces even though one side of that dispute, the federal government, gets to decide who the judges will be. This is a fundamental denial of the rules of natural justice. The first thing a law student learns is that you can't judge your own case. Fundamental and outrageous though this may be, the issue just gets a ho-hum from academics, and the politicians and bureaucrats in Ottawa just love it. But it's clearly unjust.

While the Supreme Court is the top arbiter of civil and criminal matters in the country, its most important task is interpreting laws in light of the Charter of Rights and Freedoms. In this area the power of the court is limitless with this exception: at great political peril a government can invoke the "notwithstanding" clause of the Charter and override the court's decision.

In a democracy one might think that appointments to such a powerful body—whose members hold tenure until they are seventy-five—would be done in a democratic manner. But this is but one more piece of evidence proving that Canada is not a democracy but a "soft dictatorship."

Professor Jacob Ziegel, professor emeritus of law at the University of Toronto, and one of the few academics to have given this issue more than a cursory glance, proposes two possibilities for selecting judges of the Supreme Court more democratically.

His first method would have a committee, presumably appointed by the prime minister, select a short list of candidates from which the prime minister would choose one. But one need not be unduly cynical to assume that a prime minister's committee would consult with the prime minister before making recommendations and that the prime minister's selection would be on the list. This scarcely qualifies as a bona fide reform.

Professor Ziegel's second proposal would have a joint committee of the Senate and the House of Commons "vet" any selections and have the power to recommend against any that were unsatisfactory. The obvious flaw here is that the prime minister's party would, except where there was an all too rare minority government, have the majority. Professor Ziegel likens this method to the American practice, citing the oft-times political hostility of the Senate toward the president of the day, and it is they who have the final say. There is, however, an important distinction to be made. In the United States, there is a division of powers, hence a very much watered-down version of party discipline than we have in Canada.

What both suggestions ignore are the rights of the provinces to a say. Because provinces will have to appear before the judge to be appointed in any case with the federal government, ought they not to be able to find out where the judge basically stands on the division-of-powers question in this country? Surely they must in fairness have this right if the federal government has that right.

I like the American system, which gives to the upper house, representing all of the states, the power to say "aye" or "nay" to a proposed member of the Supreme Court of the United States. It gets a bit messy on occasion, but there seems to be no lack of candidates to sit on their Supreme Court—and, after all, that process is faced by all senior members of the executive branch and by lower courts, such as the Court of Appeal, as well. Besides that, why shouldn't a person who seeks one of the highest offices in the land be questioned about his or her integrity, biases, and political background?

The problem in Canada, of course, is that the Senate is a wretched mess. Though supposed to represent regions, it is again appointed by the prime minister, and it's surely not cynical to observe that federally appointed senators are unlikely to favour their own region at the expense of Ottawa.

Throughout our history, Canadians have been pretty blasé about the Supreme Court and the federal government, with the power to appoint its members, has shown little if any appetite for reform. Moreover, Canadians, being an obedient and authority-loving lot, look at the approval process in the States and shudder.

But we'd better stop shuddering and come to grips with this august body before its grip on us means that we are governed by nine aging men and women with no mandate from the voters and who never ever must account for what they do.

How to Be a Racist

There are two surefire ways to be branded a racist in this community—criticize the state of Israel or the Nisga'a Treaty. No matter how good your "liberal" credentials—and mine are excellent—utter a word of displeasure at Israel creating self-fulfilling ambitions by settling on disputed land or whisper a word of caution about the settlement with Nisga'a and the critics jump out with a sneer on their lips, not to do battle on the issue raised, but to imply and often say that yours is the criticism of a racist. The fact that not a Jew I know believes for one moment that I am anti-Semitic counts for nothing. That I was solidly supported in my political career by the Kamloops Indian Band, its chief, and members seems irrelevant. In fact, it was the oh-so-liberal NDP that seized part of the Kamloops Indian land and crammed it into the City of Kamloops in 1973, and it is overlooked that the Social Credit government in 1976, barely weeks after taking office, returned the land.

It's a shame that important questions cannot be debated without the race card being played. Evidently we're not sufficiently mature to deal with matters on their merits. I'm going to talk plainly about aboriginal claims, Nisga'a, and native matters in general, and I'm past giving a damn about being called a racist. To start with, then, let me say this: the Nisga'a deal is a bad deal and if it passes court muster—the final decision won't likely come earlier than 2002—we're going to be sorry it did. I'd feel much more comfortable with the treaty if those who support it would meet argument with argument, but they don't—because they can't.

Without question, non-natives on Nisga'a land will not receive the same democratic rights as do Nisga'a. And I for one can understand that while the principle of one citizen, one vote is critical to a democracy, there may have to be different ways of doing that with aboriginal settlements. It would be preposterous to have non-natives living in trailer parks outvoting the natives—I have no trouble understanding that. But we must find innovative ways to provide safeguards for non-natives, and Nisga'a, to the limited extent it tries to do that, fails.

Of as much concern is the question of basic democracy on the native lands themselves. The leaders claim the systems they have are the ancient ones that their members support. But is that so? Band members feel compelled to support their elders in land claims and other allied matters because there is no alternative. To interpret this as support for the system of government they will be stuck with could be a tragic mistake. One hears far too often, especially from women and those band members who live off the reserve, that the form of government resembles feudalism more than democracy. This fatal shortcoming is compounded by the fact that the land and cash settlements are communal—which is great for the traditional leadership but by no means acceptable to the rank and file, many of whom live off native lands. Indeed many band members living on the Nisga'a land would like to have the same rights of land ownership other Canadians have.

Without question Nisga'a will have a special commercial fishery of their own. This is a race-based fishery as much as if one were granted to Italian-, German- or British-Canadians or just plain white Canadians. There is no gainsaying this—but when the issue is raised by constitutional expert Mel Smith, well known political commentator Gordon Gibson, Phil Eidsveck of the Fisheries Survival Coalition, or me, it is we who are the racists!

It's impossible to deny that this treaty permanently takes powers away from both the federal and provincial governments. The courts have consistently held that there are but two governments entitled to share the spectrum of powers in this country, the federal and provincial governments, and those powers are set forth in sections 91 and 92 of the Constitution. Yet when one points this out and reminds people that British Columbians, by nearly 70 percent with the referendum on the Charlottetown Accord, rejected aboriginal self-government entrenched in the Constitution, once more the conscience-stricken left wrings its hands and plays the race card.

Constitutionally, of course, the argument exists that, since aboriginal rights are guaranteed under Section 35 of the Constitution, this deal is simply the delineation of previous native rights now to be made formal. The point is, however, that this vexing legal argument ought to have been settled before two former Supreme Court of Canada judges, Estey and MacIntyre, cast serious doubts on the constitutionality of Nisga'a when it went before the Senate in early 2000.

Can anyone looking carefully at these issues deny they are legitimate arguments? It's not necessary to agree with either of those arguments to confirm that they are appropriate matters for public debate. How is it possible, in a democratic society, that those who wish to raise matters of principle can be shouted down by the same establishment that tried to shout them down with Meech Lake and Charlottetown?

Of course the Nisga'a and all other tribes deserve justice at long last. But as Nisga'a elder Frank Calder, the man whose lawsuit in 1972 started the native peoples down the path to settlements, pointed out, this cannot be at the expense of due process. Herein lies the tragedy. For any treaty to work over time there must be an acceptance, however grudging, that it was implemented with the consent of the people. That is not the case with Nisga'a. Indeed, as I have asserted above, while a majority of Nisga'a supported the agreement in their referendum, that majority does not necessarily support the kind of government they will be stuck with.

Nisga'a was powered through the federal Parliament like a

whirlwind—and British Columbians, native and non-native alike, will reap that whirlwind. All Canadians now watching this process from their youth, and the generations to come, will wonder just how the hell it was that such a momentous decision was made without the specific consent of their elders.

It's a serious mistake to think that the impact will be confined to British Columbia. The constitutional hybrid produced by Nisga'a will be demanded by Indian bands from coast to coast. The do-gooders and higher-purpose persons have done a great disservice to all Canadians, native and non-native alike, and we'll all pay very dearly indeed.

Because I have opposed Nisga'a and oppose any treaties that would put native self-government on the same footing as the powers of the federal and provincial governments under sections 91 and 92 of the Constitution does not mean that I oppose justice for natives, and indeed sometimes they deserve special consideration. For, quite apart from Nisga'a, there are some disturbing reminders that in the minds of the government and the courts alike natives are not ordinary Canadians like the rest of us. And my first thought when I read the press account in late 1999 of the Supreme Court of Canada's decision that aboriginal people deserved different treatment than non-aboriginals in criminal cases was that this was wrong-headed...that all were the same before the law. But something stopped me from leaping to that rather obvious conclusion. I have, you see, practiced law in areas where a lot of natives come before the courts.

I remember in Kamloops the Monday mornings in provincial court where ten or more natives would shuffle into the courtroom, all holding their trousers up because their belts had been taken from them, charged with various alcohol-related offences. Many times these were no more than common drunkenness, but sometimes they included violence, especially family violence. What struck me was the absence of non-natives. It was clear that the police patrolled the local reserve with considerable care, but what about the "better" parts of town? Were noisy parties in toney Sahali policed with the same punctiliousness as the reserve? Were the family fights in the non-native areas treated the same? How come I never ever saw a white man in that Monday lineup? Could it just be that policing methods changed from neighbourhood to neighbourhood?

I was in provincial court in Quesnel one day when an Indian was arraigned for driving on the reserve while his licence was under suspension by the superintendant of motor vehicles. The judge—a lay magistrate—asked if there was anyone from the media in the courtroom (the gallery consisting of one—me). Having determined that there were no reporters, he sentenced the lad, who had no record other than driving offences, to six months in jail! At that time the offence would always include a fine and sometimes a short jail sentence if it was a court suspension, but the police officer, who doubled as the prosecutor, demanded a stiff penalty and got it. I was so enraged that I wrote to the attorney-general but received no reply.

I'm not saying that serious crimes don't deserve serious penalties, but I *can* see how racial discrimination, applied to level the playing field, can be appropriate. While the goddess of justice is supposed to be blindfolded as she holds the scales of justice, that doesn't mean she must be stupid. Society is dealing here with enormous social problems to which society as a whole has contributed. Again, I don't mean that drunken violent behaviour can be excused if it's by a native, but it's clear that the native didn't get the same start out of the starting blocks other citizens did and did not have the same social services to fall back on. The enormous imbalance between native and non-native inmates in prison is not due to some innate, inherited factor that causes natives to offend. It clearly has sociological roots. Moreover, if policing is uneven between various communities, then that must be taken into account by the justice system. There are too many people in jail anyway. We are the second worst, behind the United States, of any country in the western world.

But I also plead the special case for special people. We have patronized and isolated native communities far too long. I know that policing has become much more sensitive since the days I left the provincial courts in the Interior, but the enforcing of law and order is still seen by many native communities as uneven.

Why, then, if I'm sympathetic to the plight of Canada's native people am I so opposed to the Nisga'a treaty? We're told that much injustice will evaporate as more and more treaties are signed. Well, so far as I can tell that hasn't made much of a difference in the rest of Canada, which has treaties. What it does tell us is that there is a terrific problem in this country involving natives and the law. Much of it stems from the clash of cultures, which sees natives trying desperately to retain their own culture while coming to grips with a much different world. Most native communities know this and are doing something about it.

But they, as our fellow citizens, need a hand—not a handout, but a hand up. Their task is not an easy one since the band lands do not usually contain enough resources to be self-sufficient, yet there is a reluctance to move off the reserve into alien territory where the attitude is not always welcoming. There is a reluctance on the part of many natives to seek education, which can only really be of assistance if they commit to leaving home forever.

There is no inconsistency between wanting the courts, and indeed society, to recognize that because we have mistreated natives in the past we must take that into account, and criticism of the Nisga'a treaty. This treaty, and others to follow, from what I can gather, will create in perpetuity a worse injustice than the policy of denying native land claims. Quite apart from the argument that Nisga'a-style treaties will constitutionalize a new form of government alongside provincial and federal governments, there is the serious question as to the appropriateness of the new governments so created.

Plenty of natives are no more happy at what's going on within present native governments than what they've endured from Ottawa and Victoria—and other provincial capitals. An interview I did in the fall of 1999, and which I'll speak more about in a moment, forces me to confess that none of us in the media have really been doing our job. Perhaps that's too wide a condemnation, but let us say that the issue of democracy on aboriginal lands has scarcely been the flavour of the month for media and politicians alike.

We've made excuses, lots of them, when you think of it. Chief molests children...huge sums of money missing...Chief and family make six figure salaries a year while rest of the band is in penury...Council election challenged as fraudulent...who dares deal with those issues? Why, it would be racist and besides, it's not all that common. Oh yeah? Who says it's not all that common? Has anyone taken an in-depth look at what's happening on the other side of the reserve boundary?

It's considered off limits to question the authority of any chief who holds himself or herself as legitimate spokesperson of the tribe in question. To do so raises anew the racist claim. It's just not done.

In the spring of 1999 the federal Liberals passed Bill C-49 giving wide expropriation powers to band councils. It brought forth the two very courageous women whom I interviewed, one a citizen of the Squamish nation, the other a lawyer. We heard appalling stories of band leaders refusing to account for millions of dollars and a rich band refusing to give basic housing to its members while its leaders live in luxury—a scene repeated throughout the country, apparently. But I want to dwell on what the lawyer told us. In essence she said this: given that Indians have lived on reserves under the paternalistic Indian Act for 150 years, how can you expect them to instantly turn into living democracies with equal rights for all? And of course you can't.

These bands have developed aristocracies. In many of them, the same families perpetually run things as surely as the aristocracy once ran England. These aristocracies were perpetuated by the Indian Agent, under the Indian Act, who liked dealing with the "devil he knew." There is little other than a veneer of democracy involved, and accountability, either for money spent or authority exercised, is often non-existent.

Treaties are being negotiated and finalized where we have only the word of those now in power that there will be representative democracy for all band members. Because we might offend the leadership we're dealing with by asking how the common folk are going to fare, because we're afraid to be seen as patronizing, we insist upon the trappings of democracy and let the ordinary folk take care of themselves. The rank and file are placed in an impossible position. If they are given a vote on a treaty, they feel they must support it, even though they'll continue to be screwed by the aristocracy for fear that a treaty will otherwise never come. The substantial percentage of Nisga'a that voted "no" or abstained in their referendum on the treaty tells us that there is considerable dissent, which I suggest is based on a distrust of the government the treaty will endorse.

The ordinary citizens of native bands are British Columbians and Canadians. They are entitled to the protection of both the provincial and federal governments, and this doesn't imply the patronizing of days of yore. What it does say is that unless and until we can be sure that band members will have a fair shake—that they will share and share alike regardless of birth or social position—our governments have not done their job.

If there had been a history of democratic government on reserves over the decades, the senior governments would be entitled, and indeed required, to honour decisions of their leadership. But—thanks to white man's laws—there is no democratic tradition. Many native leaders say their citizens don't want our system but prefer their own. Well, to quote a famous lady of the '60s—Mandy Rice-Davies of the Profumo scandal fame—"They would say that, wouldn't they." After all, it is they who will profit from the continuation of that system.

Our governments have an obligation to those fellow citizens we have forced to live under an oligarchic government, patronized by authority under the Indian Act, to ensure that the type of government they get is not just suitable to their leaders who gained power under the Indian Act, but meets with the approval of all who must live under it. The federal government, far from ensuring that minimum standard, has in fact, through Bill C-49, made sure that the ruling classes on the reserves have even more tools at their disposal to exercise ironclad rule over the people they govern.

We therefore betray aboriginals twice—once by putting them on reserves subject to the patronizing and corrosive rule of Big Brother, then later, when we abolish the reserves, leaving them with inadequate or no democratic institutions in place.

There is racism involved in the handling of aboriginal affairs. There has been since the beginning. But sometimes, what is called racism by some is really some common sense, which, if applied, would eliminate the injustices that governments have inflicted on aboriginal peoples. And sometimes racism is the only defence open to those whose consciences and, dare I say it, bleeding hearts, have prevented an open and fair discussion of aboriginal issues.

NOT NEW, PROBABLY NOT
A PARTY, AND CERTAINLY
NOT DEMOCRATIC

The NDP is certainly not new. It was formed in 1961 to incorporate the old Cooperative Commonwealth Federation (CCF) into a newer party, including elements that had not necessarily felt comfortable with what was to many people a sort of agrarian reform movement. For this reason, it may also be difficult to call it a party in the traditional sense although it is, I admit, merely a matter of semantics.

But they are semantics important to the NDP, so perhaps a moment can be spared on the point.

When I was a member of the Social Credit government of British Columbia back in the '70s, the NDP delighted in calling us a coalition, which somehow called into question our legitimacy to say nothing of our integrity. We were a coalition on the make, seeking power for power's sake; they were a movement that had integrity and would forsake the easy route to power in order to safeguard sacred principles of socialism. Yet, in truth the NDP was formed deliberately as a coalition of groups that all traditionally saw themselves and were seen as part of the left but were often at cross purposes at election time and often spent as much time fighting each other as the enemy. But the point is an academic one really. At the same time, the Social Credit party was probably a much more honest reflection of the right wing of the spectrum than either of the traditional parties, the Liberals and the Tories.

All parties are really coalitions. Many times your membership in a party depends on where you were born more than any philosophical commitment. I've met Tories who I would have said were very much in the centre and in fact were left wing. The runner-up to Joe Clark in the Tory leadership race of 1999 was David Orchard, who sounded a lot more like a member of the NDP than anything else. For one thing, he was and remains bitterly opposed to free trade, which was the centrepiece of Tory policy in the 1980s and remains so today. Many Liberals are much further to the right than most Tories and any who know Roy Romanow, the premier of Saskatchewan, know how uncomfortable he would be with the B.C. New Democrats.

Is the New Democratic Party democratic? The litmus test for that surely must be how they conduct conventions, especially leadership conventions, and when compared to the way most other parties, save the federal Liberals, conduct such things, the NDP fails the test.

The Parti Québécois is probably the most democratic as they were the first to allow all their members to vote electronically. So, now, does the Canadian Alliance and the Liberal party of B.C. Even the national Tories, redundant though they may be, in 1999 moved to electronic voting by all members selecting Joe Clark over David Orchard and several other easily forgotten wannabes.

The old B.C. Social Credit Party—very much to be distinguished from the Alberta or national parties—was also democratic. Or very nearly so. Each constituency sent twenty-five delegates and the only automatic delegates were the MLAs. The non-democratic part was that delegates from constituencies far removed from the site of the convention were at a financial disadvantage.

It's quite a different story with the NDP in British Columbia. Somewhere between 25 and 30 percent of the delegates are "institutional." They get their status because of membership in trade unions, or women's groups, or young New Democrats and so on. Even federal MPs get status in what is supposed to be a provincial "wing." These people are not elected from the party but selected from a component part of the party. Then we get to the constituency delegates. The party permits twenty-five delegates per constituency organization but also allows bonus delegates for larger constituency memberships. This means that the more populated Lower Mainland and southern Vancouver Island ridings get a big boost, which is compounded by the problem "up-country" voters have in affording to get to the convention. Moreover, not only do MLAs have automatic delegate status, so do MPs.

This is what makes it so difficult to predict the outcome of an NDP leadership race. For example, in the February 2000 leadership convention, the president of the B.C. Federation of Labour and other "institutional" delegates didn't announce their intentions beforehand so the media were left to guess where their support will go.

There is a case, of course, for loading the delegates from bigger constituencies. If, in golf parlance, the deal is match play, where each constituency is equal, then sparsely populated areas have a potency beyond their numbers. On the other hand, if there are seventy-five votes in the legislature, why shouldn't the source of those seventy-five voices be equal?

I don't suppose I would be writing this were it not for the fact that the NDP have always claimed a monopoly on virtue. To hear them in full-flighted oratory one would think there was a direct connection between the NDP and the democracy of ancient Greece and that everyone else is descended from Attila the Hun. The fact is that not only are the NDP not especially virtuous in their makeup, the scandals of the NDP in B.C. are such that the sins of others pale into insignificance. There are, indeed, no finer speeches on the requirement that a minister resign if under a cloud than those delivered by the NDP in opposition to Social Credit. It must be recorded, however, that those principles evidently were not meant to bind the NDP when in power.

But to the NDP, there has never been any division between the federal wing and the provincial. Yet there clearly is, judging by Roy Romanow's quite different brand of socialism in Saskatchewan, which is really a pragmatic middle of the roadism when contrasted with the federal party and the labour-dominated party in British Columbia. Indeed the federal party, from which all left wing direction is expected to flow, is in deep trouble.

The basic question is, given the modest provincial success of the NDP, how is it that the Labour party in Britain first tasted power seventy-five years ago and our version of the left, the NDP, hasn't had a sniff?

There are substantial historical reasons, of course. When the Conservatives, in that famous meeting at London's Carlton Club in 1922, broke up the coalition with the Liberals, it exposed a very fractured Liberal party, one faction led by Lloyd George, the other by Asquith and the alternatives for the British voter were quickly reduced to Labour and Tory. The Liberals haven't recovered to this day. But for all that, the Labour party had to make severe structural changes before it could be seen as a viable alternative to the Tories.

The first Labour prime minister, Ramsay Macdonald, damn near destroyed the Labour party when in the late 1920s he entered into a "national government" with the Tories who, in the next election, swamped the Labour party and only indulged Macdonald as premier for a couple of years. The post-war Labour governments of Attlee, Wilson, and Callaghan were more protests against the Conservatives than voter affection for Labour, and it wasn't until Tony Blair won in 1997 that Labour really won its own mandate on its own terms.

The NDP should look at why that happened. How did Labour suddenly become the party of the centre-left where most voters are?

It did this by reinventing itself from the bottom up. The major move was removing the stranglehold the Labour unions exercised over the party.

This wasn't easy. It probably killed John Smith, the leader who had most to do with it. And it may have cost Neil Kinnock the 1992 election. But it did the trick, and when Blair took over he had a party that the labour unions had no alternative but to follow even though their influence therein had been drastically reduced.

Can the NDP accomplish in Canada what Labour did in Britain? Can it become a modern social democratic party and elbow the Liberal party out of its traditional territory on the left and even capture some of the centre? I somehow doubt it. In early 1999, Alexa McDonough, leader of the NDP, made some noises about doing this and then Canadian Labour Congress president Bob White dumped all over her, pleading to the troops that while reforms should happen they ought not to be imported from other countries. Decoded, that says, "If you think you're going to do what John Smith, Neil Kinnock, and Tony Blair did to their unions and kick us out of the driver's seat, think again, lady."

In the August 1999 policy convention, the NDP, far from examining themselves with any care and perhaps questioning their close connection with labour, decided to recognize the special nature of Quebec (without investigating any of the ramifications) and supported a special tax on short term-market investments—the "Tobin Tax"—as the way to deal with globalization! For such a tax to be effective, every country in the world that had any sort of stock or commodities market—or for that matter might have one—would have to agree to go along. Their naiveté was enough to take one's breath away!

Certainly it can be fairly said that the NDP leadership in Ontario and British Columbia, where they must revive their fortunes both federally and provincially, shows no sign that the leadership is prepared to tackle big labour head on. Indeed, if anything the unions have even greater clout than ever. Even though unions have lost ground with diminishing membership, their leaders have spooked the NDP into believing that all union people vote NDP. They don't. Not by a long shot. There has always been a strong "conservative" vote amongst union members. I can tell you from my own political experience as a Social

Credit candidate that this is true. In 1975, one of my strongest polls was in Logan Lake, then peopled almost exclusively by unionized mineworkers in the nearby Highland Valley and their families. The largest union-dominated poll in the riding, North Kamloops, supported me both in 1975 and again in 1979.

In February of 2000 the B.C. NDP held a leadership convention to replace the fallen Glen Clark. It sounded like something from the early 1900s. There was an ode sung to Joe Hill, the murderer who was executed in 1915 in Utah and thus became a martyred hero for the left. All candidates extolled their labour union connections, though that was pretty tough for recent arrival Gordon Wilson. He made a valiant effort and the name most mentioned was not any of the leaders but Tommy Douglas. One felt that the ethereal voice of Keir Hardie, the founder of the British Labour party, might permeate the room. Not a whisper of reforming the party, not a thought expressed about modernization.

As it stands now, the NDP is in worse trouble than it has ever been. It's true that Alexa McDonough engineered a small electoral comeback in 1997, but it really wasn't much. Of greater worry is that the NDP owe much of its caucus to the personal popularity of the MPs. Take Kamloops, for example. That is not a NDP constituency but Nelson Riis is very popular. Svend Robinson, Lorne Nystrom, and Alexa Mcdonough are also examples where the popularity of the MP outruns the popularity of the party by a wide margin.

To win a chance at government, Alexa Mcdonough must take on Ken Georgetti, the president of the Canadian Labour Congress, a very tough cookie indeed. I don't think she has the jam to do it, and I'm not sure she could win if she tried. Thus you can count out the NDP for some years to come.

Buzz Hargrove, Ken Georgetti, Bob White, and other labour leaders are wrong—the solution to the NDP's problems does rest in the British example. Until the New Democratic Party does what other parties of the left have done and cuts the formal bonds with organized labour, it will remain firmly in the political Land of Nod. Names after awhile lose their meaning. No one cares now that Tory is an old Irish Jacobite term that, during the American Revolution, meant you lost your land at best and were probably tarred and feathered to boot. The Radical Socialists in France are neither radical nor socialist.

Likewise the NDP is not new, not really a party, and certainly not democratic. But then no one really knew what Social Credit meant either. To the credit of the Bennetts and their followers, no Socred ever pretended to know, being content to be generally speaking on the right of the spectrum and quite prepared to listen to all others who felt the same. To them the name, quite properly, was meaningless and irrelevant.

The NDP lose because their specific policies are outdated and appeal to no one except a small minority that think the world ended when Tommy Douglas died. And they lose because no one forgets that they say they're socialists—and everyone remembers that socialists are utterly irrelevant to the world today.